PRAISE FOR *A Deadly Misunderstanding*

"This work is truly exceptional as well as inspirational. There is no issue that is as significant today as the relation between Islam and the West. The author provides a precious balm for the wounds that need to be healed."

> —Dr. Seyyed Hossien Nasr, University Professor of Islamic Studies at George Washington University and author of *Understanding Islam*

"I believe passionately that Siljander has discovered a real pathway here—a means to open dialogue that we have not seen in centuries."

> —Dr. Ergun Caner, dean of the Divinity School, Liberty University

"This is very good work Siljander has been doing: building bridges, looking on what unites us as humans, and addressing our fears and prejudices with rational argument and love."

> —Dr. Yasir Suleiman, professor of Modern Arabic Studies, King's College, Cambridge

"An engaging story, sure to surprise and inspire many."

> —*Publishers Weekly*

"I have experienced firsthand the strategy underlying Mark Siljander's book: that loving our enemies has the power to counter the threat of religious extremism."

> —Hon. Tony Hall, former U.S. Congressman, U.S. Ambassador to the U.N. Food Program and three-time Nobel Peace Prize nominee

"Resolving existing hostilities between Muslims and Christians will require that we deal with the ideas behind the guns. This book does a masterful job of pointing the way."

—Dr. Douglas M. Johnston, president and founder
International Center for Religion & Diplomacy

"A Deadly Misunderstanding is an incredibly important work in the field of ideology change related to terrorism and war. It represents hope for the integration of civilizations in a world much too fixed upon the clash of civilizations."

—Rod A. Beckstrom, coauthor of *The Spider and the Starfish*

"Extremely well-researched and the product of enormous thought. This book demands to be read."

—T. Davis Bunn, visiting teacher at Oxford University
and award-winning novelist

"Christians who read *A Deadly Misunderstanding* will gain insight not only into Islam but into the way of Jesus as well. They'll also find themselves unable to put the book down: it's a real page-turner, and its message is revolutionary."

—Brian McLaren, author of *Everything Must Change*

"I have been privileged to witness Mark D. Siljander's pioneering efforts. Each page of *A Deadly Misunderstanding* is a testimony of Mark's willingness to study, struggle, and pay the price necessary to see Jesus' Way of reconciliation and transformation restored to the Church and society."

—Gary P. Bergel, president, Intercessors for America/
Heritage Harvest International

A Deadly Misunderstanding

A Congressman's Quest to Bridge

the Muslim-Christian Divide

Mark D. Siljander

with John David Mann

Foreword by Ban Ki-moon

HarperOne

An Imprint of HarperCollinsPublishers

HarperOne

HarperCollins books may be purchased for educational, business, or sales promotional use. For information please write: Special Markets Department, HarperCollins Publishers, 10 East 53rd Street, New York, NY 10022.

HarperCollins Web site: http://www.harpercollins.com
HarperCollins®, 📖®, and HarperOne™ are
trademarks of HarperCollins Publishers

FIRST EDITION

Designed by Joseph Rutt

Library of Congress Cataloging-in-Publication Data

Siljander, Mark D.
A deadly misunderstanding : a congressman's quest to bridge the Muslim-Christian
divide / Mark D. Siljander with John David Mann. — 1st ed.
p. cm.
Includes bibliographical references and index.
ISBN 978–0–06–143828–8
1. Islam—Relations—Christianity. 2. Christianity and other religions—Islam.
3. Religions—Relations—History. 4. Islamic countries—Relations—Europe.
5. Europe—Relations—Islamic countries. 6. Conflict management—Religious aspects.
7. Islam and world politics. I. Mann, John David. II. Title.
BP172.S556   2008
261.2'7—dc22   2008006590

08 09 10 11 12 RRD (H) 10 9 8 7 6 5 4 3 2 1

Contents

Foreword

We live in troubled times. All around us, intolerance and religious tensions are on the rise. Extremist dogma is gaining ground, and moderate voices are being undermined. Every day brings new instances of the harmful impact cultural misunderstandings can have on relations between communities, both within countries and across national borders.

The greatest schism appears to be between followers of Islamic and Christian traditions. Many of today's global challenges—though mostly political in nature—are being aggravated and rendered intractable by this worrying development.

Many column inches are devoted to bewailing this trend, yet few individuals have taken active steps to address it. With this important new work, Mr. Siljander has courageously stood up to be counted. A man of deeply held faith and conviction, his journey began in the halls of the U.S. Congress and took him from meeting rooms at the United Nations all the way to the back alleys of Beirut and the shifting sands of the Sahara. Along the way, he engaged with academics and clerics, statesmen and stateless men, and scores of ordinary Christians, Jews, and Muslims on the meaning of their faith and traditions. Throughout, he also devoted countless hours to a close textual study of the holy books of the great religions.

A Deadly Misunderstanding chronicles this journey of discovery and presents Mr. Siljander's simple yet powerful insights. For instance, he explains that the term *Allah* is simply the Arabic word for God. Thus "some twenty million Christian Arabs pray to Allah every day, and Jesus himself . . . used the nearly identical Aramaic version of the word, *Alaha,* when he spoke about God."

Through his scholarship and his sojourn, Mr. Siljander builds a compelling case that any faithful reading of religion and its teachings should serve to unite, not to divide. He documents what many of us instinctively believe: that people of the great faith traditions all share the same core beliefs and ideals; that compassion, solidarity, respect for life, and kindness toward others are but some of the many common threads tying together men and women of faith.

Today, there is an urgent need to rebuild bridges and to enter into a sustained and constructive intercultural and interreligious dialogue, one that stresses common values and shared aspirations. It is my fervent hope that *A Deadly Misunderstanding* helps jumpstart this much needed conversation.

Ban Ki-moon
Secretary-General, United Nations

On the Green Line

With its glamorous history, mix of European and Arab influences, and liberal, cosmopolitan culture, Beirut had once
been known as "the Paris of the Mideast." But those days were
long past. There was no mistaking the street where I stood: we
were in the center of a war zone.

It was the fall of 1982. Israeli troops were poised all along the
country's southern border, ready to go in and wipe out the Pal-
estinians, who were dug in along that same border and determined to repel the Israelis at any cost. It was a standoff ready to
explode at the smallest spark. I had just spent an hour visiting
Camille Chamoun, the eighty-two-year-old Christian former
president of Lebanon, hoping to get his read on the situation.
The conversation had been inconclusive.

Chamoun's house was located on the Christian side of the
barren strip of scorched earth that divided Beirut into its two warring, irreconcilable halves: East and West, Muslim and Christian.
The desolate strip of land had been dubbed, with an irony I'm sure
nobody intended, the Green Line. I'd never seen anything less
fertile, less evocative of life, less *green*, than this parched place.

We emerged and stood for a moment, blinking under the glare
of the Mideastern sun and chatting with our Israeli security
guard, when suddenly a shot rang out.

I should have ducked, but instead I froze. This was only my second trip to the Mideast, and I hadn't yet acquired the war-zone reflexes that would come in the years to follow. Like a carpenter's calluses or coal miner's cough, a kind of hair-trigger vigilance comes with the territory, part and parcel of the seasoned diplomat's trade. In central Africa, you learn how to cope with mosquitoes; in Beirut, you learn how to duck bombs and bullets. But as a freshman congressman just learning the ropes, I was pretty green myself, and I was still staring dumbly at the rubble-strewn streets, looking vaguely for the source of the sound, when I was grabbed and yanked roughly to the ground—and a sharp *pinnnggg!* rang out, tearing a small cloud of dust from the wall just inches from where my head had been. The young Israeli dragged me ten or fifteen feet to a bus, pitched me in, and jerked the door closed. Palestinian snipers were closing in.

With the sound of my heartbeat pumping in my ears, one thought flooded through my racing brain: *What the hell am I doing here?*

Once the danger passed, I stayed on and surveyed the area for a while, climbing through the rubble, hoping to catch a clear glimpse of the PLO forces on the other side of the Green Line, the Muslim side. At the time, I didn't realize what a vivid metaphor this effort was for the direction the rest of my life would take.

Suddenly I caught movement out of the corner of my eye, and the next moment I was staring into the barrel of an Uzi. I had stumbled onto an Israeli lookout post hidden among the rubble, and a young Israeli soldier, having no way of knowing who or what I was, was about to blow my head off. Nobody was reading anyone any Miranda rights here—this was war, kill or be killed.

My reflexes were a little sharper this time, and fortunately I had learned a bit of Hebrew since my first trip to the Mideast some months earlier. I knew just enough to shout out, "B'vaka sha, ani esh-congress!" *Please, I'm a congressman!* The boy's finger froze on the trigger, and he slowly lowered his Uzi.

In a few short hours, I had nearly been killed twice, and whether delivered by a bullet from the Christian side or Muslim side of that deadly Green Line, my death would have been just as final. No matter which side of an armed conflict one supports, both sides are ultimately sponsors of the same end: destruction.

This is not a book about Beirut, but it is a book about a world rift by its own Green Line, split like a macrocosmic Lebanon into two warring, seemingly irreconcilable halves. More particularly, it is about the efforts of one man, clambering about the rubble straddling that pervasive Green Line, to peer over at the other side and see what ground the two sides might possibly share.

THIS WAS NOT the path I set out to follow twenty-five years ago, as a conservative Republican congressman and Evangelical Christian just entering the world of Washington politics. At the time, I believed that Islam was a religion of violence, that the Qur'an preached the destruction of all non-Muslims, and that the Qur'an and Islam were of the devil, as godless as the great evil of communism whose defeat was then the defining purpose of American foreign policy. I believed that Islam and Christianity were contradictory at their core, that the Eastern Islamic and Western Judeo-Christian cultures were irretrievably opposed to one another, and that the only possible solution to this conflict was the conversion of "them" so they would come to think like "us." My worldview could not have been clearer or simpler—or more myopic.

In the years that followed, I was led to question the truth of these axioms. In time, I learned that every one of them was utterly, categorically false. I learned that when we stop buying into our cultures' prejudices, assumptions, and prevailing habits of thought and begin to investigate the texts of our different holy books in their original languages, conflicts between crucial terms and entire passages that have traditionally been viewed as irreconcilable begin to evaporate.

I learned that the deadly misunderstanding dividing our world today need not do so tomorrow.

What follows in these pages is not some new form of ecumenism or syncretism where Christians, Muslims, or anyone else is expected to give up cherished and long-held beliefs or creeds. It is rather a chronicle of one person's search for a rich common ground that exists between these faiths and cultures. It has been a constant source of both astonishment and inspiration to find that this common ground is not some far-fetched ideal but is textually sound and eminently practicable. In some extremely delicate and hostile political situations, I've seen it work miracles.

Mark D. Siljander

Hostage

One day in the fall of 1983, as I prepared for a speech at a rally in Washington, D.C.'s Lafayette Park in support of Soviet Refuseniks,[1] I received a visit at my congressional office on Capitol Hill.

My secretary informed me that there were two gentlemen to see me, one from the FBI and the other from the CIA. As she ushered them into my office, I noticed that the FBI agent carried a bulky briefcase. The two men explained who they were and the reason for their visit: there were some "concerns" related to my speech that week.

"Fact is, Congressman," said the FBI agent, "we were hoping you'd reconsider."

Reconsider? I wasn't sure what he meant.

"Reconsider your participation in the event." He glanced at the CIA man, who clarified: "We'd like you not to give the speech."

The CIA agent explained that his agency had received word that Yasser Arafat was less than pleased with the position I was taking on Soviet emigration policies.

Actually, elaborated the FBI guy, Arafat had put out a contract on me.

I was flabbergasted. Why would Yasser Arafat want me dead? Why would he even care about some insignificant young freshman representative from Michigan?

The FBI guy said, "We don't think it's about the length of your tenure, Congressman."

"It's the passion of your words," continued the CIA guy, "that has caught the attention of certain people."

"Well, I'm not canceling my speech," I replied, "contract or no contract. I'm not letting some thug dictator hold me hostage!"

They must have expected that would be my response, because they didn't seem at all surprised. The FBI agent opened his briefcase, reached in, took out a bundle of fabric, and held it out to me. It took me a moment to realize what it was: a bulletproof vest. They wanted me to wear it when I gave my speech. "Wanted" is probably the wrong word. It wasn't a suggestion.

They handed me the vest, got to their feet, advised me that they were assigning me a twenty-four-hour armed security detail until the rally was over, and left my office without another word.

After they left, I sat fuming. When the CIA agent had said, "It's the passion of your words," I knew exactly what he was talking about, and knowing that Arafat was somewhere out there trying to silence me only intensified that passion.

Earlier that year I had sponsored a joint resolution "expressing the sense of Congress regarding the reduction of emigration from the Soviet Union" (H.J. Res. 279). The "evil empire," as Ronald Reagan had dubbed the Soviet Union, was clamping down on Jews wanting to emigrate to Israel, and I was angry about it. That "sense of Congress" was, in a word, *outrage*.

During these early years in Congress, my worldview was decidedly one-dimensional. Despite holding advanced degrees in political science, my interest in world affairs boiled down to one simple ideological goal: we had to defeat the Soviet Union. My Republican congressional colleagues and I saw the world as falling into two neatly defined groups: those aligned with us and those aligned with them. Based on the philosophy "the enemy of my enemy is my friend," we regarded anyone who was against the Soviet Union as "freedom fighters," and we did everything we could to help their cause around the world. Anyone who was aligned with the Soviet Union we called "terrorists." Back then, we had no clue what a genuine terrorist was.

My simplistic view of world affairs extended to my position on the Mideast. The dictates of both my party and my religion said that we should be 100 percent pro-Israel—I had my rationale, but never mind the reasons—and that was pretty much where I stood. During my tenure in the House of Representatives, in multiple speeches, in committee meetings, on the floor of Congress, on television, in every venue and at every opportunity, I denounced the Soviet Empire and warned of the threat to America. These diatribes typically included a list of people we saw as being linked with the Soviet Union—the immoral and brutal tyrants of the world. Along with Castro, Qaddafi, and a host of others, Yasser Arafat was one of the chief names on that list. In our view, Arafat was an assassin, a revolutionary, and a criminal.

Interestingly, we didn't mention Saddam much in those days. He was obviously a pretty bad character, but we were content to quietly support him as long as he was making trouble for the Iranians. We didn't quite know what to make of the Iranians; they perplexed and unnerved us.

MY ENTRY INTO Congress happened to coincide with the aftermath of the first Islamic revolution in modern times. In 1979, the Ayatollah Ruhollah Khomeini had overthrown Mohammed Reza Pahlavi, the autocratic and modernistic (also corrupt, brutal, and American-backed) shah of Iran, and established an Islamic state—which expressed its fury at the West when a group of militant students stormed the American embassy, taking dozens of American hostages, and holding them captive for 444 days.

The events in Iran had shocked America to its core. Hearing this religious leader in the Mideast call *us* "the Great Satan" was disturbing and confusing. The fact that we seemed power-less to do anything about it was even stranger and scarier.

In his nationally televised debate with incumbent Jimmy Carter, candidate Ronald Reagan asked the American people, "Are you better off than you were four years ago?" This was os-tensibly a question about our national financial condition—but domestic policy and household economics were only the surface issue. It was the numbing nightly news reports on the fifty-two American hostages in Iran that offered the most eloquent reply to that question. The hostage situation cast a pall over our every-day affairs, serving as a constant reminder that our primacy in the world was not as secure as we had assumed. The Iranian hostage crisis was on everyone's mind, yet few of us compre-hended its implications for the future.

Still, when I arrived at Capitol Hill in the beginning of 1981, I had given little serious thought to the situation in Iran or to Arafat. I had no intention of becoming involved in the affairs of the Mideast, or anywhere else outside the United States, for that matter. As a young first-term congressman, my interests lay in serving my Michigan constituency and helping my Republican colleagues gain the upper hand on Capitol Hill. After defeating Jimmy Carter the previous fall, Ronald Reagan had tapped Michigan representative David Stockman to join his new cabinet as director of the Office of Management and Budget (OMB). A special election was held to fill the vacancy, and in January 1981, I found myself moving from Three Rivers, Michigan, to the sub-urbs of Washington, D.C.

In the early months of 1981, the hostage crisis was over and done with, resolving almost magically during the new president's first moments in office, and as I began settling into my new Washington post it was a thrill to participate in some small way in the new administration's triumph.[2] Shortly after arriving in D.C., I attended a reception for several of the hostages who had just been returned to America.

The hostage reception was at a posh suburban home in northern Virginia. I took a seat on a couch next to Malcolm Kalp, one of the former hostages, and listened as he described his captivity. To my surprise, he spoke less about his own ordeal and more about his struggle to grasp the thinking of his Muslim captors.

"We still think the Soviet Union is our enemy," he said, "that worldwide communism is still the principal threat to our way of life. But the real challenge isn't the Soviet Union—it's militant Islam." He glanced over at me with a haunted look and added, "We have no idea what we're up against."

I left the party feeling shaken.

For the next few years I didn't have much time to think about Malcolm Kalp. I was too busy trying to help Reagan's new conservatives, the first generation of Washington neocons,[3] take back control of the Hill from the Democrats, who had controlled both houses of Congress for years.

As the new kid on the block, I was fortunate to make friends quickly with a number of congressmen who would go on to deeply influence American politics for the next two decades. The press called us the "Young Turks"—Newt Gingrich, Tom DeLay, Duncan Hunter, Jack Kemp, Vin Weber, and a handful of others. We were on fire with our vision for a renewed Republican party, a vision that focused domestically on tax reform and an economic program later called Reaganomics, and internationally on strengthening and deploying our military, with a goal of defeating the Soviet Union. We were prepared to further these goals as aggressively as necessary.

In 1982, I was approached by a cadre of high-profile Evangelical Christian leaders who wanted me to accompany them on a fact-finding mission to Israel and Lebanon. When I politely declined their invitation, they asked me to reconsider. "We need a congressman to help us get in to see the Israeli prime minister and the Lebanese president. Frankly, we need a politician to give us cover."

"International relations is not really something my constituency is all that concerned about," I explained to them. "I represent a white, rural community in Michigan. My interests are in middle America, not the Mideast. There are no Middle Eastern people in my district. I think a Palestinian person owns our local Big Boy—and he didn't even support me!—but that would be about it."

But they persisted. Eventually I relented and agreed to accompany them that summer to the Middle East, having no idea that this was only the first of dozens of trips to the world's many hot spots. Soon, despite my insistence that I had no aspirations to be a traveling diplomat, my international portfolio began to grow. A few months after that first Mideast trip I was sitting on the Foreign Affairs Committee, then on the Mideast Subcommittee. Soon I was appointed Republican chairman of the Africa Subcommittee, under whose auspices I traveled to South Africa—where civil unrest and active resistance to apartheid were reaching a fever pitch—and later made a documentary on the situation there.

Part of the reason for this growing involvement in foreign affairs was a knack I seem to have for languages. I'm not a linguist and have never set out to learn foreign languages for their own sake, but I've always liked connecting with people. In addition to English and Spanish, I can find my way at a basic level in Hebrew, Korean, and Mandarin Chinese, and given a few days in-country, can manage in French, Italian, and Portuguese. Arabic and Aramaic would later be added to this list.

Before I knew what was happening, this conservative Christian white Republican representative from a rural agricultural district in western Michigan was embroiled in international relations to the point of being noticed by my nemesis, that communist-sympathizing, rabble-rousing trouble-maker Arafat.

THE REFUSENIK EVENT at Lafayette Park came and went. I delivered the speech safely, my bulletproof vest discreetly hidden under my suit jacket. Whether Arafat's hit had been lifted or simply went awry (or was bogus intelligence in the first place), I'll never know. But if the hit had lifted, my sense of outrage had not, and the incident only deepened my enmity for the man and everything he stood for.

Arafat lived another two decades, and our paths would cross again many years later—face-to-face, and in an altogether unexpected way. But just a few weeks after the Refusenik rally, my attention was brought back to the situation in Lebanon, not because of Arafat but because of a sobering new turn in world events.

On October 23, 1983, shortly after six in the morning, a yellow Mercedes delivery truck entered the grounds of the Beirut International Airport, where U.S. Marines were temporarily housed, then abruptly accelerated, crashing through the barbed wire perimeter and barreling into the lobby of the marine headquarters. The explosion reduced the four-story cinderblock building to rubble, killing more than two hundred inhabitants. The simmering threat that Malcolm Kalp had warned of had now erupted, and I was soon on my way back to the Mideast.

The suicide attack on the marine barracks in Beirut was devastating. The blast was followed twenty seconds later by an identical attack on the French barracks. The death toll included 241 American servicemen, fifty-eight French paratroopers, and six Lebanese civilians. It was the deadliest single day for the U.S. Marines since the battle of Iwo Jima, and remains to this day the deadliest overseas attack on Americans since World War II.

But it was more than an awful, isolated tragedy; it was also a critical turning point in the global tension between East and West. It was not the first suicide bombing of a U.S. encampment in the Mideast; six months earlier, on April 18, a suicide attack at the U.S. embassy in West Beirut had killed sixty-three. And it certainly was not the Pearl Harbor of this conflict; that place is held by the September 11, 2001, attacks eighteen years later. But the Beirut marine barracks bombing was the watershed event through which our modern era of suicide bombers and militant Muslim terrorism announced itself. It destabilized our sense of security (some would say complacency), and it reinforced to a seismic degree a set of cultural and religious prejudices that were already well entrenched in Western society. From that point on, there was a clear and concerted effort in Congress to promulgate a view that equated "Arabs" with "terrorists." The Soviet Union's star was in decline; we had a new enemy.

Having already been to the Mideast several times, I was recruited to join some of my colleagues in an effort to help buoy up the troops' morale in Beirut during Thanksgiving. When we arrived, we found the American forces utterly demoralized. The depth of the horror we encountered there in the midst of the wreckage, with the stench of death still in the air, made an indelible mark on my emotions. It was both horrifying and heartwrenching. This was no act of war; this was a senseless, ruthless mass murder. The Iranian hostage crisis had been nationally humiliating, but this was worse. They weren't just kidnapping us—now they were killing us.

ONCE A YEAR, in February, a series of special events takes place in Washington, D.C., called the National Prayer Breakfast. The president and vice president are normally in attendance, along with hundreds of senators and congressmen and as many as four thousand friends and colleagues.

The National Prayer Breakfast dates back to the 1940s, during World War II, when a handful of senators and congressmen began meeting informally to give each other personal and spiritual support. Over the years, loosely defined ground rules evolved: Though the members meet in the name of peace and in the spirit of Jesus Christ, they need not be Christians to participate; all members are welcome, regardless of political or religious affiliation. The meetings are off the record, without political context and for purely personal purposes. The group met quietly, without press or public notice, for a decade.

One day in 1953, soon after he was sworn in as the country's thirty-fourth president, Dwight "Ike" Eisenhower was speaking privately with a friend, Senator Frank Carlson. He confessed that he found the White House the loneliest place he had ever experienced. Carlson invited him to come join their prayer group. That year, Ike attended the first combined House and Senate Prayer Breakfast, and the event has continued ever since.

There is a whole range of associated events during the week of the Prayer Breakfasts, including special lunches on that Wednesday and Thursday, each typically attended by several thousand people. One of these, the Diplomatic Luncheon, emphasizes guests from the diplomatic corps; the other is an International Luncheon, with a focus on foreign affairs and visiting dignitaries and heads of state. These are not specifically religious events. They are meant to provide a forum where men and women of common dedication can come together in unity and help foster the cause of peace in the world. Usually a congressman or senator reads a passage from the Bible—typically a general inspirational message that would not offend the non-Christians in attendance—and one or more outside speakers gives a talk. Billy Graham spoke there every year until the age of eighty-two, when illness prevented him from attending.

The annual event is a source of great inspiration for many, and it has served as something of a model for the kinds of international reconciliation processes that some of us would later explore. But at one particular National Prayer Breakfast event in February 1984, just months after my visit to the marine barracks in Beirut, I was not inspired but outraged. The speaker was not Billy Graham but a visiting Muslim dignitary from the Mideast who addressed the assembled guests with a reading from the Qur'an.

The Qur'an! I couldn't believe it. It felt like a betrayal, and I was genuinely alarmed at what I saw as its sinister implications. Walking out of the International Luncheon, I stepped out of the D.C. Hilton and into the freezing Washington weather to pace the streets in a mix of anger and confusion.

Of course, I had never actually *read* any of the Qur'an. In those days, I wouldn't have even considered picking up a copy to browse—it would have felt like heresy. Besides, I didn't need to: I already had ample evidence that Islam was a religion of violence and that the book from which it drew its inspiration was the devil's work. My Evangelical Christian friends had been warning of Islam, the "sleeping giant," for years. I'd never paid much attention to the details, but I got the general picture. After all, I had sat on a couch with Malcolm Kalp. And stood in the wreckage of the marine barracks in Beirut. And worn a bullet-proof vest, in case Arafat's reach *did* extend all the way to Lafayette Park. What more evidence does a person need?

What had begun as a simmering sense of mistrust and unease now boiled over as white-hot righteous indignation. It was bad enough that Americans had been held hostage in Iran and blown to bits in Beirut. Now we were willingly submitting ourselves to the rabid rantings of militant Muslims—willingly submitting ourselves to being held hostage at our own National Prayer Breakfast in our own capital! It was just too much.

From my office I dashed off a stinging letter of protest to the leadership of the National Prayer Breakfast. What did they think they were doing, I wrote, allowing a Muslim leader to read the Qur'an at an event supposedly dedicated to peace and brotherhood? Were they crazy?

MANY YEARS LATER, after the September 11 attacks on the World Trade Center and the Pentagon, when Christian leaders began denouncing Islam and the Qur'an from pulpits and radio stations across America, their litany of vitriol and hysteria was both frightening and yet oddly familiar.

When a well-known American preacher went on *60 Minutes* and denounced the prophet Muhammad, the founder of Islam, as "a terrorist,"[4] when another prominent American clergyman told thousands of Christians at a convention in Dallas, "We are on God's side: this is not a war between Arabs and Jews, this is a war between God and the devil,"[5] when a high-profile Evangelical Christian leader appeared on the *NBC Nightly News* and declared that "the God of Islam is not our God . . . I believe it is a very evil and wicked religion,"[6] I remembered my letter of protest to the National Prayer Breakfast leadership. It was *my own voice* I recognized.

Back in 1984, what I didn't realize was that I was also a hostage, held captive by my own ignorance and fear—much like the fear that has held so much of the world hostage since the events of 9/11. And while I could not have remotely suspected it at the time, that same letter of protest would trigger a series of encounters that would eventually shake me loose from the beliefs that held me there.

Paradigm Crash

In 1986 I suffered my first political defeat in twenty years.

Up to this point, my career had seemed almost charmed. At the age of twenty-one, I won my very first seat in local Michigan politics by a single vote. I won my seat in Congress through a campaign that had no chance of winning, according to the experts. Now, after winning fourteen races in a row and serving three successive terms in the U.S. House of Representatives, it seemed almost a given that I would continue to serve in the House for many years to come. This confidence would soon prove unfounded.

When I came to Washington in 1981, the media dubbed me one of the biggest Jesus freaks ever elected to Congress. The reason those Christian leaders had singled me out to accompany them to the Mideast was my reputation for being a committed Evangelical Christian myself. I was so outspoken about my religious views that some degree of controversy followed me everywhere I went. But the notoriety had never been more than mild; by and large I had always experienced my faith as a political strength. Ironically, though, it was my religious convictions—or, more accurately, the media's portrayal of them—that broke my winning streak and forced me to go looking for a new professional path.

We were running a decent campaign in the spring and summer of 1986; Reagan was in his second term, and the Republican party had gained tremendous strength. Our tracking polls showed us as having 84 percent or 82 percent, as low as 70 percent in some places—but hey, it only takes 51 percent to win. Still, in politics you can't afford to assume anything. My staff noticed that the Christian community, which normally included my strongest supporters, was somewhat quiet that summer, and we weren't getting the volunteers we needed. Someone on my staff said, "Let's make a short audio tape and get it out to all the pastors, get them stirred up to turn the people out to vote."

This was just a week or so before the primaries, so a script was hastily written and sent to my office on the Hill. As I sat reading through it, I felt uneasy. It had been written by my press secretary, who was very religious, and it sounded a little extreme, even to me. I came to one section and was thinking, *Should we rewrite this?* when word came that I had to go for roll call. Congress was trying to end its summer session and there were votes yet to complete. I voted, came back to my office, and sat down again with the script.

My chief of staff came in and said, "Mark! We have to get this thing recorded—it's all set up and ready for you!"

I hesitated. There was a section that talked about fasting and praying, about "breaking the back of Satan." I thought it was over the top. "I don't know . . ."

"It's okay, it's good," my chief of staff urged. "Hey, if we want to get this duplicated and distributed, we have to record it now!"

Instead of listening to my instincts, I let myself be swayed by my pride and the pressure of the moment. We made the recording; the cassettes went out. One pastor who received a copy thought it sounded absolutely crazy and gave it to my opponent, who heard the portion that talked about "breaking the back of Satan" and went nuts. This was meant in a spiritual sense, but he took it (not unreasonably) as an ad hominem attack. The press agreed. A few days before the election the headlines hit:

Siljander Calls Opponent "Satan"
Siljander Gone over the Edge
Siljander Calls for "Prayer and Fasting" for Himself

There was nothing we could do. There was no time to explain, no time to take out more ads, no time to make public appearances and respond. Too many of our supporters sat on their hands, the opposition flooded the polls, and I lost the nomination. My political career was over.

Most congressmen lose their seats in the November elections, when the fall session is practically over, and don't have to face their colleagues. This was not the case for me. I had lost in the primary, the first Tuesday after the first Monday in August, and there was still nearly half a year left to serve. I had to go on through January of the next year, pretending I was still a congressman, sitting in session, voting, and going through the motions. Thus it was that my career in Congress ended, to borrow the words of T. S. Eliot, "not with a bang but a whimper."[1] It was torture.

THAT JANUARY, AS the humiliating final days of my last term were whimpering to a close, I received a visit from a man named Doug. My 1984 letter of bitter protest had set in motion a series of three encounters with three friends—almost like Ebenezer Scrooge's Christmas Eve visits from the three spirits in Charles Dickens's *A Christmas Carol*—and Doug was the first of these. Over the next few years, these encounters would shake the foundations of my worldview, starting with something I thought I knew inside and out: the Bible.

Doug's name is not known to many. He keeps a quiet profile, yet he is arguably one of the most influential people I've ever met. He knows more senators and congressmen in the United States and more heads of state around the globe than most, and he has both their ear and their respect.

Doug has since become an important mentor in my life, but at the time, I knew him only slightly. Though Congress runs the National Prayer Breakfasts, Doug has much to do with what goes on the agenda, and because I saw him as more or less the de facto head of the event, I had addressed my stinging polemic to Doug. He had never responded to my letter, and true to form, he has to this day never come out and told me exactly what he thought when he received it. But I suspect he said to himself something like, "Well, this young Christian congressman doesn't understand much about the world, does he?" And the way I'd managed my 1986 reelection campaign certainly proved him right in that assessment.

Now, on this fine frigid morning in January 1987, as I sat wondering what to do next with my life, Doug came to my office on Capitol Hill and asked if he might visit for a bit.

"Of course," I said.

We chatted for a few minutes, and then he got to the point: if I didn't mind his asking, as a follower of Jesus, what was my strategy in relation to other people in my travels around the world? I replied without hesitation: it was to convert them to the Christian faith. He nodded thoughtfully, then asked a deceptively simple question: "And why is that?"

I was taken aback. Why would he ask such an elementary question? "Well," I began, "of course, converting people to the Christian faith is the basis of Jesus's teachings. It's our duty as Christians. It's . . . what we do. You know this, Doug." Silence. "I mean, it's in the Bible."

"Really." He paused and fixed me with his gaze. "Would you name one verse?"

Now I was baffled. Was he serious? This was first-grade Sunday school stuff! "Doug, come on. What are you driving at?"

"No, really," he pressed gently. "Go ahead. Just one."

Okay, I thought, *if you insist. Let's see* . . . And a moment later I was stunned to realize that I could not bring a single verse to mind—not one. I felt humiliated.

I considered the famous verse from the end of Matthew's Gospel, the Great Commission: "Go, therefore, and convert all nations, and baptize them in the name of the Father and of the Son and of the Holy Spirit" (Matt. 28:19).[2] But Jesus here makes no direct mention of "Christianity" or of a specific religion. In John's Gospel, Jesus says, "No man comes to my Father except by me" (John 14:6), but here again, he makes no mention of Christianity or of any particular religion.

In the Acts of the Apostles there is the story of Peter's great sermon in Jerusalem, soon after the "tongues of fire" Pentecost, in which he urges the Jews to "repent, therefore, and be converted, that your sins may be blotted out" (Acts 3:19). It is one of the most famous New Testament passages containing the term "convert." But be converted *to what*? Peter didn't specify.

I looked at Doug and weakly said, "I'll get back to you later with that verse."

AFTER DOUG LEFT, I began combing through the Bible, determined to find the answer, and I continued to comb, not for an evening or a week but for a *solid year*. I searched the entire New Testament high and low, looking for personal vindication, until I finally arrived at the disturbing conclusion that it simply wasn't there. The strategy of converting people to Christianity, a strategy that I had so fervently held as a God-given, biblically based mandate, was never mentioned in the Bible—not once.

I consulted my Webster's Dictionary. It defined "Jesus" as "the founder of the Christian religion," and informed me that "Christianity" was "the Christian religion, based on the Old and New Testaments." But were either of these statements true? I could not find a single verse in the entire New Testament that stated or even implied that Jesus of Nazareth promoted, began, or intended to begin any religion. In fact, he never once mentions the word "religion" in the Gospel writings, nor does the word "Christianity" appear anywhere in the text of the Bible.

Although Jesus himself does not refer anywhere to any religion, James, Jesus's brother and the early church's first leader, does. In fact, he provides a definition of his own, quite different from Webster's: "A pure and holy ministry before God the Father is this: To visit the fatherless and widows in their affliction, and to keep himself unspotted from [i.e., unpolluted by] the world" (James 1:27). Hardly an elaborate belief system or highly structured dogma.

The book of Acts reports that the followers of Jesus were referred to in Antioch as "Christians," but this apparently was used as a term of derision. The word "Christian" appears only three times in the entire Bible, and never as a term these disciples applied to themselves. What did they call themselves? "Followers of the Way." Again, hardly a term denoting an exclusive creed or complex code of conduct.

When Gentile believers began to join the Jewish followers of the Nazarene's teachings, the group's leaders debated hotly whether these newcomers should be required to follow the crucial precepts of their own religion, namely, Judaism. The circumcision question was critical: in order to be part of the group that followed Jesus, must non-Jews become Jews? Did they need to "convert," in the sense that I had always understood the word?

The conclusion, of course, was no. Following Jesus, according to Jesus's own disciples, was not a matter of religion; it was about the revelation of God's truth as conveyed by Jesus's influence on the human heart. As I continued poring over the text, I came to an inescapable conclusion: the teacher from Nazareth *never intended to start a religion.* What he was creating was a *movement,* a relational revolution of the human heart.

So where did this leave Christianity? Where did it leave *me*? I thought of myself as a devout Christian—but what did that really mean? Was it an illusion? Had I been brainwashed? I felt a victim of my culture, heir to a long tradition of assertions by countless articles and books, teachers and preachers, about truths they all insisted were in my holy book. I had accepted what I had heard.

An even more unsettling thought occurred to me: if I had been misguided on this critical strategic point of my faith, were there other areas where I was just as misinformed? Was my personal mission in life based on erroneous information? Was my faith based in truth—or was it a blind faith? All at once my belief system felt incredibly fragile. It was as if the ground I stood on was crumbling under my feet. As devastating as it had been to lose my reelection campaign, this was worse.

I thought of the phrase "paradigm shift," which had been coined by social scientist Thomas Kuhn in the 1960s and was just starting to enter popular usage at the time. But the term seemed to pale next to the intensity of the experience. This was not a paradigm shift. This was a paradigm *crash*.

AT ABOUT THIS same time I also experienced a parallel paradigm crash in my professional life, when I came face-to-face with the appalling limitations of modern diplomacy.

Within six months after leaving office, I was appointed by President Reagan as an ambassador to the United Nations. My wife, Nancy, and I moved to New York City with our two-year-old daughter, Elizabeth, and newborn daughter, Laura, and that September saw the beginning of a new chapter in my career in government. Though the position I held was termed alternate delegate, it was a full-fledged, Senate-confirmed ambassadorial rank. I would serve on U.N. committees, make speeches on the floor of the United Nations, and represent my nation within the world community. It sounded incredibly exciting.

In reality, it proved to be fairly frustrating. Unlike being in Congress, as a delegate you can't just get up and start talking on the floor of the United Nations, and when you do talk, you can't necessarily say what you think. As I soon learned, everything a U.N. delegate says in session first has to be passed by the State Department, because there are potential international ramifications to every uttered word. And the committee meetings seemed like little more than countless hours of fruitless discussion.

By this time I was passionate about world affairs and eager to contribute my efforts toward peace and stability around the globe. Serving as an ambassador to the United Nations, the heart of global relations, should have felt like a dream come true. Instead it felt hollow. Was I really doing any good?

A few weeks into my term, the State Department asked me how the new delegate was enjoying his position. "Frankly," I admitted, "this job is pretty boring. What I'd really like is to do a lot less committee work and instead meet one-on-one with a series of delegates from around the world." They agreed, and so for the last few months of 1988, I spoke with forty-one "permanent representatives" from forty-one nations around the globe, meeting with each one individually over lunch or dinner. In these meetings I asked them about themselves and their lives; about their region of the world, what it was like, and what were their biggest challenges; and finally, what did they think the United States could do to improve our image in the United Nations and around the world?

These seemed to me like pretty basic relational questions, the things anyone would ask. You can imagine my shock at their responses. Every single one of these representatives, down to the last man and woman, ended our lunch or dinner by saying some variation of the same thing: "You know, Mark, in all the meetings we've had, all the time we've spent in New York, you are the only diplomat so far to ask me a single question that goes deeper than the weather or the state of Manhattan traffic."

The first time I heard this I laughed, assuming that he was kidding. The second and third time, I shook my head and said, "You're joking," but they told me, no, it was absolutely the truth. I still didn't believe them—but then I heard it a fourth time, and a fifth, and a sixth . . . *and a fortieth*. By the forty-first time, I was aghast.

They said they were absolutely amazed that someone cared what they thought about these issues. When I asked them what transpired in their other conversations, they said, "We don't have *conversations*. The United States tells us how they suggest we vote, what they suggest we do. They're cordial and friendly, and very polite. But they don't ask us anything about ourselves or our countries, and certainly don't ask for our opinions on how the United States can better its relations around the world."

I went to the weekly U.S. mission briefings and asked, "What's going on? If we don't even talk to these people, what the hell are we doing here?"

One man sighed almost inaudibly, his face expressionless. It was our permanent representative, General Vernon Walters. "We're not here to make friends, Ambassador Siljander, we're here to try to maintain a modicum of stability in the world. This isn't summer camp; it's global diplomacy. We don't want to appear weak."

Of course, I thought. No wonder we struggle so in our efforts to effect diplomatic solutions around the world. No wonder we're increasingly hated around the world. No wonder international conflicts continue to rage, seemingly without any end in sight. *We don't want to appear weak.*

Something was profoundly wrong here, and I had the sense that I'd just stumbled over what it was. It was the *interpersonal relationships* that were missing. We weren't engaging with these people, person to person. We didn't do it in our junkets as congressmen, and we weren't doing it in our dealings as professional diplomats either.

Sitting there in the State Department official's office, mute with shock, I remembered an encounter with Richard Nixon a few years earlier.

IN THE EARLY 1980s, the Young Turks had hit on the strategy of using something called Special Orders to promote our neocon agenda. By requesting the time in advance, any member of Congress has the right to stand on the floor after the regular session is over and hold forth on whatever topic he chooses for up to an hour. We would put in such Special Order requests in groups, so that when one of us reached the end of his hour, the next would stand up and take it from there.

What made this powerful was a fairly recent invention: C-SPAN. Everything we said was broadcast to tens of thousands of people (and eventually, to millions). We kept this going for hours every night, talking about tax reform, the Soviet Union, our new vision for the Republican Party, and how we could take over Congress if we did it right. We kept this up for years.

Nixon took notice of our strategy and thought it was pretty sharp. In 1986 he invited us over to his room at the Madison Hotel in D.C. It was called the China Room, made for him in 1972 as the place where he would meet with the Chinese premier, the principal site of the greatest diplomatic victory of his career, and now it was where he met with us: Newt Gingrich, Jack Kemp, Vin Weber, Duncan Hunter, and me.

He said he really respected what we were doing and that we were the future of the Republican Party, the future leaders of the country. Then he went through the country, state by state, telling us who would become governor, who would become senator, how Reagan would fare in the next election—and looking back years later, I saw that he was absolutely right in nearly every single case. It was uncanny. Whatever else one might think of

Nixon, he was a brilliant tactician, like a walking computer, and he had every election pegged.

And then he said something that has stayed with me through all the years since: "In the end, boys, it's our interests that count. It's never a matter of trust. Not reliability, morals, none of that— it's whatever serves our interests, that's what counts in the end."

NOW, FRESH FROM my personal encounters with forty-one delegates from around the world, I remembered Nixon's words with a chill: *It's never a matter of trust—it's whatever serves our interests.*

Right then and there, sitting in that State Department bureaucrat's office, I had an epiphany: *the whole world follows that principle.* It wasn't just Nixon. That's politics. That's diplomacy. And that's religion. Conversion. Coercion. Diplomatic pressure, economic incentives, demonstrations of military readiness, political leverage, proselytizing, politicizing, policing, propagandizing . . .

The United States tells us how they suggest we vote, what they suggest we do.

Suddenly the principles of international diplomacy didn't seem much different from the principles of religious conversion: *adopt our ways, come over to our way of thinking and serve our interests . . . or else.* If this really was the foundation of how the different peoples of the world were going about relating to each other, we were in serious trouble.

Was that really what my religion, my party, and my country were all about? And where in all of this were the actual teachings of Jesus?

THREE

The Secret Language of the Bible

In the summer of 1990, the Lebanese Parliament and Lebanon's new president agreed on constitutional amendments that divided parliamentary power evenly between Christians and Muslims, and that country's fifteen-year-old civil war finally began drawing to a close. But even as a period of relative calm settled over Lebanon's Green Line, the tectonic pressures of East-West hostilities were about to erupt elsewhere in the world.

A few years earlier, following eight years of war with each other, Iran and Iraq had both turned their attentions to Lebanon, using that troubled state as a staging ground for their own proxy scuffle (much as the United States and the Soviet Union were doing at the exact same time in nearby Afghanistan), Iran supporting the Muslims and Iraq supporting the Christians. Now, as the conflict in Lebanon calmed down, Iraq refocused its military energies and resources in yet another direction: on August 2, Saddam Hussein's forces poured over Iraq's southern border into Kuwait.

The United States quickly responded with protective measures known as Operation Desert Shield. The following January, Desert Shield became Desert Storm. A decade of simmering anti-Islamic sentiment in the West and anti-American rhetoric in the East began heating up. We were at war—and because of it, I began receiving almost daily communications from the second of my "three visiting spirits," a man named John Booko.

John is the founder and pastor of an interdenominational church in the little town of Three Rivers, Michigan. I'd known him since my early twenties, and we remained close even after I moved out East in 1981. Shortly after I began my first term in Congress, my father died. At the still tender age of thirty, I badly needed a father figure, someone I could look to for advice and mentoring. John said, "I'll adopt you as my son," and I have considered the Bookos my father and mother ever since. When Nancy and I were married in late 1983, just days after my return from the devastated marine barracks in Beirut, John officiated at our wedding. (Actually, John officiated over the five other ministers and rabbi who all participated in the ceremony. You could say we were really *thoroughly* married.)

There are two more things you need to know about John Booko. The first is that he is an American-born Assyrian. The Assyrians are descendants of one of the oldest civilizations in Mesopotamia. Some three thousand years ago, they were the dominant force in that part of the world, with a rich culture that excelled in astronomy, jurisprudence, the arts, architecture, medicine, and the natural sciences. More than a millennium later, though no longer a major player in the region's balance of power, Assyrians made history by becoming the first people to follow Jesus of Nazareth as their national faith in A.D. 179, more than a century before Armenia. There are some five million Assyrians in the world today; they account for the majority of the roughly one million Christians in present-day Iraq. John's grandfather was a priest of the Assyrian Church of the

East, and both his parents were born in northern Iraq. John has also authored two books on the role of Assyria in biblical prophecy.

The second thing about John is that he is passionate about world affairs—and fearless. In April 1985, John accompanied me on a trip to Egypt, where we had the opportunity to meet with Hosni Mubarak in his presidential palace. John had met Menachem Begin in Jerusalem a few years earlier and had been looking forward to meeting Mubarak ever since.

After a bit of polite small talk, John turned to Mubarak and said, "You know, Abraham was from Ur of the Chaldees. That means he was an Assyrian. I'm an Assyrian. Since Abraham is your father, that also means I'm your father—but it also means I'm father of the Jews as well. Now, here's what I'd like to do: I'd like to pray for peace between you and Israel."

I couldn't read Mubarak's expression, but it was clear that the American ambassador who had accompanied us was about to have a fit. Here's an Evangelical Christian pastor, albeit an Iraqi Assyrian, offering to pray for a Muslim president—and saying all these weird things about Abraham. This was way beyond State Department protocol, and the poor ambassador looked like he couldn't decide whether to scream or faint.

Without waiting for a reply, John stood up and began to pray. Nobody else moved. When he had finished, he sat back down. Mubarak took a breath to speak, and the ambassador visibly flinched.

"I loved that," said the president of Egypt, and he leaned over and gave Pastor Booko a big bear hug.

John grinned. "I did the same thing with Begin, and he hugged me too."

John's bold pastoral gesture of rapprochement in Egypt made a deep impression on me, and years later it would serve as a model for our experiments in diplomacy through personal friendship around the world.

Now, in 1991, as George Bush (senior) went to war with Saddam Hussein and Desert Storm broke over the sands of Kuwait, John became intensely focused on following the unfolding events in every last detail. He called me or e-mailed me at least daily, asking what I knew about the latest developments. And in the course of our conversations, he began talking to me about a topic that continues to fascinate me today: Aramaic, the "secret" language of the Bible.

FEW IN THE modern West have ever even heard of Aramaic— or hadn't until 2004, when Mel Gibson startled Hollywood with the news that he was shooting his new film, *The Passion of the Christ*, mostly in this ancient tongue.

Gibson's reason for the unconventional choice was simple: Aramaic was the language Jesus and his contemporaries actually spoke. The words recorded in the New Testament, though they were written down in Greek, would have been spoken mostly in Aramaic. Indeed, while the vast majority of Christian scholarly thought insists that Greek was the original language of the New Testament, a small but growing group of contemporary scholars believe that the earliest Greek-language versions of the New Testament may well have been translations of Aramaic originals long since lost.

Aramaic survives today as a spoken language in small Assyrian communities in the Mideast and the United States, and John had undertaken a serious study of the language. As he and I conversed about current events, I told him about my conversation with Doug and my search for a viable origin for the doctrine of conversion, and he urged me to secure a copy of the New Testament in Aramaic. The only way to legitimately pursue the question, he said, was to try and get a clear sense of what the authors of the New Testament were actually saying—in the words, phrases, and idioms they would have used.[1]

There is quite a bit of scholarly debate about whether the Aramaic version was derived from the original Greek or the other way around, but for our purposes, it really doesn't matter. Either way, John explained, the Aramaic version would most accurately let us into the mindset and perspective of a first-century Middle Easterner through its cultural norms, nuances, metaphors, and figures of speech.

When Eastern thoughts are translated into Western languages, such as Greek, Latin, or English, there is enormous potential for mistranslation. It is not simply a mechanical process of replacing one term with another. It means lifting a body of meaning completely out of its original cultural context and placing it into a foreign way of thinking.

For example, suppose we read in an article today, "The senator was enjoying himself at the party, but he left looking rather blue." Someone not familiar with English idioms might be alarmed: was there something wrong with the senator's blood oxygen? Was he gravely ill? An American, of course, would know that the word "blue" also has another meaning: "sad" or "depressed."

But wait—suppose the article was translated directly into German. The German word for "blue," *blau,* has another meaning too, only in German the secondary meaning is not "depressed" but "drunk." To the German reader, the sentence would appear to make perfect sense, but he would come away with a very different impression of the senator!

And this example compares two similar contemporary cultures. Translate from the language of one culture to a profoundly different culture, and the possibilities for confusion escalate alarmingly. When General Electric translated its slogan "We bring good things to life" into Mandarin for a promotional effort in China, it came out, "We bring your ancestors back from the grave."

In such trivial examples, the errors are humorous and entertaining. When they involve pivotal beliefs that entire civilizations are willing to die for—and to kill for—it becomes quite serious indeed. I immediately sensed that John was onto something important, though I didn't yet grasp just how important.

John then showed me an example of the potential for mistranslation drawn from the actual Aramaic of the New Testament. Many of us are familiar with the famous saying of Jesus, "It is easier for a camel to go through the eye of a needle than for a rich man to enter the kingdom of God" (Matt. 19:24, NKJV).[2] It is pretty obvious that a camel cannot make its way through the eye of a needle—it's not *difficult* or *unlikely*, but flat-out *impossible*. The meaning of the metaphor should be perfectly clear: rich people cannot enter heaven—period. And for two thousand years, Christians have dutifully tended to equate poverty with purity and money with sinfulness. Which is a shame, considering that conditions of continuing poverty have exacerbated disease, personal misery, and social strife for untold millions around the globe.

But is that really what Jesus said? Let's consult the Aramaic. In the language Jesus spoke, the word for "camel" is *gamla*—but this word also means "rope." And here the subtleties of culture and idiom come into play. When buying thread, if a Middle Eastern woman comes upon a sample that is too thick, she will typically make the comment, "This is a rope!" A "rope" in this context does not necessarily mean a literal rope, but rather denotes a somewhat coarse thread.[3] Can such a thread fit through the eye of a needle? Absolutely. It's a little more difficult, and takes some care in the doing, but it is certainly doable. Perhaps Jesus did not mean rich people are all doomed to suffer for eternity—only that it might take a bit more care not to let the accumulation of riches taint one's soul.

I soon found another example, this one with more profound implications. In a long-debated passage in Luke, Jesus says:

If anyone comes to Me and does not hate his father and mother, wife and children, brothers and sisters, yes, and his own life also, he cannot be My disciple. (Luke 14:26, NKJV)

How can Jesus instruct us to love our enemies in one breath, and in the next tell us to hate everyone dearest to us? Christian theologians have labored mightily over the centuries to explain away this blunt contradiction.

Again Aramaic provided an answer. The word in Aramaic for "hate" is very similar to a word meaning "set aside." With that one substitution, the passage suddenly makes complete sense, fully consistent with the rest of Jesus's teachings: devoting one-self to God would certainly mean *putting aside*, or holding as a lesser priority, one's family, friends, possessions, and even one's own life. Not "hating" them—just keeping them in perspective.[4]

If such simple examples could so profoundly shift with the meaning of a single word, what other possibilities might this "secret language" hold in store? I excitedly searched out a copy of the Peshitta, the earliest known Aramaic New Testament (dating back to the third or fourth century), along with its 1933 translation into English by Dr. George Lamsa, a scholar of Iraqi origin himself.[5] Armed with several Aramaic dictionaries and the Lamsa Peshitta, I began to dig in.

FROM MY YEAR of searching through the Bible after that en-counter with Doug, I knew that the word "convert" appears ex-actly ten times in the New Testament (King James version) and five times in the Old Testament. A close read of the Aramaic edi-tion turned up several words that are normally translated into English as "convert," the most common being *shalem*.

This was fascinating. It sounded very similar to the Hebrew *shalom*, which means "peace." *Jerusalem* is "the city of peace," and Jews today greet each other with a *shalom alechum* that means, "Peace be with you." Aramaic and Hebrew are both Se-mitic languages and are closely related. Was there a connection?

Indeed there was: the meaning of the two words is virtually identical. In the New Testament, Jesus often greets others with a simple "Peace be with you," which in his Aramaic vernacular would have been *shlama loch,* based on the same word, *shalem.* (Listen carefully to Mel Gibson's film and you'll hear James Caviezel in the title role saying "Shlama loch" numerous times.)

But now I was confused. If the word means "peace," then why was it being used in some passages where the English says "convert"?

As my linguistic investigation deepened, I learned that the word *shalem* has another meaning: "submit" or "surrender." In ancient times, cautious travelers in the East, wishing not to draw attention to themselves lest they fall prey to robbers, would open their hands in a surrendering posture when encountering strangers on the road, to show that they had no weapons and only peaceful intent. "I come in peace" equals "I submit to your goodwill." From this meaning, by the way, we derive our modern word "salute," along with the modern Western practice of the open handshake and the Far Eastern corollary, the bow of submission. Over time, the word *shalem* accrued a whole range of meanings, including "greeting," "peace," "salute," "turn back," "complete," "fulfill," "surrender," "submit."

Reading on, I felt my excitement growing. This was starting to make sense!

When Peter told the crowd, "Repent and *be converted*" (Acts 3:19), the word he used was *shalem.* His literal meaning was not, "Give up your religion and adopt ours instead," but something more like, "Turn back from your sinful ways and *surrender yourself* in faith to God."

Continuing through the Aramaic text, I soon found another word with a meaning similar to *shalem* that is also translated into the King James's English as "convert": *punaya,* meaning "turning" or "restoring." The term is often used in reference to "turning" Gentiles away from polytheism, and in another form, *p'na,* it is used especially with Jews, urging them to *restore* their faith or *turn back to* the one true God. Thus, at the very end of the book of

James, when the author speaks of "converting the sinner" and saving his soul (James 5:19–20), the Aramaic word is *p'na*, which translates more accurately as "be restored from *error*." James is not talking about convincing non-Jews to become Jews or non-"Christians" to become "Christians." He is talking about helping troubled Jews return to the simplicity of submission to their faith. *Repent and be converted. Submit to God. Be at peace.*

It was crystal clear from the text that neither Jesus nor any of his followers ever advocated that anyone "convert" from one religion to another. Every use of the various Aramaic terms meant the same thing: "submit," "surrender," "return," "be fulfilled," "be restored." Our insidious concept of conversion was a linguistic error, a clear mistranslation. Pure and simple: *a mistake.* A deadly misunderstanding.

I set the book down and drew a deep breath. Finally, here was a solid answer to Doug's question. Where did that strategy of conversion come from? From a terrible distortion of Jesus's words. Instead of being a process of personal revelation and redemption, conversion had become a tool of oppression. Perhaps this erroneous interpretation came with Constantine's declaration in A.D. 325, which made "Christianity" the official religion of the Roman empire. Or maybe the true meaning had already been lost years before, a casualty of the perennial human tendency to divide and dominate—the pernicious impulse to create a Green Line between "us" and "them."

However it happened historically, and however innocent or willful the motives, the idea had been twisted: the original notion that Jesus and his followers promoted, of *conversion* as something personal and transformational, had in time become dogmatic and political. And the seeds of centuries' worth of violence had been sown. *It's never a matter of trust,* as Nixon had put it; *it's what serves our interests.*

•   •   •

IN 1992, THE Cold War officially came to an end following the collapse of the Soviet Union on Christmas Day 1991. A little over a year later, on February 26, 1993, Americans awoke to unthinkable headlines. Shortly after midnight, a lone Ryder truck exploded in the basement of Tower One of the World Trade Center in lower Manhattan, killing six and injuring more than a thousand others. It had been almost exactly a decade since the Beirut marine barracks bombing. The violence had come to American soil.

When I heard the news that morning, Malcolm Kalp's words came flooding back in all their chilling accuracy: *The real challenge isn't the Soviet Union—it's militant Islam. We have no idea what we're up against.* Now we were starting to find out.

The paradigm of global politics that had shaped those early years in Congress was obsolete. George Bush (senior) was talking about a New World Order, but what I was sensing was a New World Conflict. The world seemed to be hurtling toward an inevitable confrontation between militant Muslim extremists and the West, and I could not see any force on the horizon equipped to stop it.

The years during and after my tenure at the United Nations had been an extremely active time. I produced two radio commentary programs, "It's Your America," which was heard over several hundred U.S. stations, and "Asia in View," which was broadcast throughout Asia in English and Mandarin Chinese. Nancy and I had arrived in New York in 1987 with two children; we soon had twice that number (Allison Marie was born in 1989, Mark Jr. in 1991). In an effort to find ways to support my growing family as well as my deepening interest in foreign cultures, I expanded my consulting company, brokering various negotiations, both governmental and nongovernmental, as a sort of private-sector diplomat and mediator. This provided us with a fairly steady income—and even more, it provided a steady stream of opportunities to travel overseas, where I could continue strengthening and expanding my sphere of global contacts.

As much as I was doing, I wanted to do more. I wanted to be genuinely effective, to contribute more substantially to finding true solutions to this terrible escalation of global tension.

Being an ex-congressman opened all sorts of doors. Despite being on my own now (which meant, among other things, that I needed to cobble together my own funding for trips), I could still travel to places and meet people that most citizens never could. I often traveled as an "emissary" of the bipartisan House Prayer Breakfast Group, of which I'd been a member since 1981. But I wondered if perhaps returning to the Hill as a sitting congressman would allow me to accomplish more. In 1991 I made a bid for another seat in Congress, this time representing Virginia. *Maybe that 1986 defeat was just an anomaly,* I thought. *Maybe I can recapture that momentum, get my old game back, recover that string of political victories.* But it was like trying to go back through a door that had shut and bolted behind me. The election bid failed.

Clearly, whatever was in store, whatever it was I was supposed to do next, would lie on a new path, not an old one. Perhaps this new path would lead to a much more meaningful future than I could ever find through elected office. But if the door behind me was impassable, all those in front seemed just as tightly locked. I had not yet grasped that the Aramaic language my mentor had shown me might be the key that would begin unlocking those doors.

The Other Holy Book

Soon after the first World Trade Center bombing, I received the third and last of my three paradigm-crashing visitations, this one from a man from Nepal named Charles Mendies. Nancy and I had known Charles for years. He and his wife, Susan, who are both Nepali, travel quite a bit, especially throughout southern Asia, and are well acquainted with prime ministers and heads of state all over the world.

Years earlier, Charles and Susan had worked at an orphanage in Kathmandu called Mendies' Haven. In 1989 the Supreme Court of Nepal convicted Charles of preaching Christianity—which had been banned in Nepal for over thirty years—and sentenced him to six years in prison. Charles's conviction and incarceration for helping orphans and putting Bibles in hotels brought worldwide attention to the Nepalese persecution of Christians. Within a year Nepal passed a new constitution that guaranteed freedom of religion, and Charles was freed.

Not long after his release, Charles had a conversation with Doug very much like mine. Charles had been dedicated to "fighting the good fight" and converting the world to Christianity. Doug asked him the same question he asked me: "Why?" The conversation had quite an impact on Charles, whose approach to people of different faiths mellowed considerably.

Charles was in D.C. not long after the 1993 bombing in Manhattan, and we got together to talk about our lives and the state of the world. I told him a bit about my search in the New Testament for a justification of conversion, and he nodded. I described my discoveries about Aramaic, about *shalem* and *punaya* and the meaning behind the English word "convert," and coming to the conclusion that Jesus had never meant to start an exclusive religion but rather to describe a state of one's personal being in relation to God. After going on for a while, I paused to gather my thoughts, and Charles suddenly spoke up. "You know, Jesus is mentioned extensively in the Qur'an."

It caught me completely off guard. The Qur'an? This seemed the most ridiculous thing I'd ever heard. I didn't believe him for a moment and told him so.

He gave me a withering look and said, "Mark, you're so westernized and Christianized. You need to educate yourself."

For days, the comment rankled. Not long before, a longtime Christian friend of mine named Jim Lawler had utterly mystified me by saying that he had read the Qur'an—which was shock enough—and that doing so had "strengthened his faith." I'd known him since grade school days; we used to call him "Crazy Jim." Now I thought he was just being his usual Crazy Jim self. Not Charles, though—I thought Charles was being cocky.

I'll bet he hasn't really read it himself, I thought. This is how these exaggerations get started: someone takes something out of context, passes it on, it gets distorted, and before you know it you have educated people saying Jesus is a key figure in the Qur'an! Give me a break. It was so annoying, in fact, that I felt compelled to do something. I had to prove that Charles was wrong—and there was only one way to do that.

Which is how it happened that on a chilly evening in the spring of 1993, I stood on the sidewalk outside a bookstore in Reston, Virginia, pacing and talking to myself, probably looking for all the world like someone trying to get up the nerve to ask his boss for a raise or a girl out on a first date. But it wasn't a raise or a date I was steeling myself to go after—it was a book.

To me, it felt like a struggle for my soul. Back and forth I argued with myself as the sky darkened. Only a few years earlier, I would never have even considered purchasing a copy of the Qur'an, let alone bringing it into my house. This was the devil's book we were talking about here! Why would any sane person want to spiritually contaminate his home?

But if I didn't go and read it myself, how would I know? Of course, Charles was wrong—but how would I *really* know?

It was approaching 9:00 p.m. The store was about to close. I went inside, picked out a copy, and paid for it.

Sitting in my study at home half an hour later, I unwrapped my parcel, placed the book on my desk, and stared at it. Then, a flash of inspiration: maybe there was an index! That would certainly allow me to get the job done quickly. A quick look in the back of the book—and so there was. *Excellent. I'll just look through the pages back here, let's see . . . H . . . I . . . J . . .* —I stared at the page, incredulous. There was "Jesus," followed by page numbers for the entries. Dozens of them. It would take me hours to look them all up.[1]

I turned to the first entry and (not realizing that my actions transgressed Islam's injunction against defacing the holy book) began underlining and highlighting.

THE ARABIC WORD *qur'an* comes from the shared Arabic and Aramaic root *qara'a,* meaning "to read" or "to recite."[2] According to Muslim tradition, this was the command the angel Gabriel gave three times to Muhammad when he confronted him in the Hira cave, a few miles northeast of Mecca in A.D. 610. Muslims believe the Qur'an, "the Recitation," is the final revelation from Allah, given to his last and greatest prophet. The Qur'an is divided into 114 sections or chapters, called *suras,* which are in turn divided into verses, or *ayas.*

The more suras and *ayas* I read, the more amazed I became. The text talked about Adam and Eve, Cain and Abel, Abraham, Mount Sinai, Noah, Solomon and Sheba, Moses, heaven, Satan, hell, angels, end times, Judgment Day, sin, forgiveness, Zechariah, John the Baptist, and Mary, whose name adorns an entire chapter.

And Jesus. Boy, did it talk about Jesus. Charles hadn't exaggerated; if anything, he'd understated the case. Jesus—or Isa, as he is called in Arabic[3]—is mentioned in the Qur'an more than 110 times, ninety directly and twenty or more indirectly. He is called "righteous," "pure and without sin," the "Word of Truth," the "Word of God," the "good news," "intercessor," "mediator," a "witness for Allah," a "straight path," and the "right path to follow." He is referred to as "the Messiah" eleven times. The Qur'an says that Isa performed miracles, healed the sick and the lepers, breathed life into clay, and had the power to raise the dead. It says that he will return again on Judgment Day.

In the years to come I would learn a great deal more about Jesus and Islam. For now, it was sufficiently astonishing to find that the carpenter from Nazareth was not only "mentioned extensively" in the Qur'an, as Charles had put it, but that he clearly played a unique and highly revered role there.

For that matter, so did the Bible itself. I had expected to read excoriations of Jews and Christians and derision of their holy books at every turn. Instead, I kept bumping into passages where the Qur'an mentioned the holy books of both Jew and Christian and gave them a place of honor. It was captivating. I began underlining these and soon started an index of my own. By the time the last page was turned I had totted up over one hundred references asserting the validity of spiritual truths in the al-Turat (Torah), Zubor (Psalms), and Injil (New Testament)! For example:

And We gave them The Book which helps to make things clear (sura 37:117). And He sent down the Turat (Torah) and Injil (Gospel) before this, as a guide to mankind (sura 3:3–4). We gave Moses the Book (sura 2:87). Each one believeth in Allah, His angels, His books and His messengers. "We make no distinction . . . between one and another of His messengers" (sura 2:285). Those to whom We have sent The Book study it as it should be studied (sura 2:121). We believe in Allah, and the revelations given to us, and to Abraham, Ismail, Isaac, Jacob, and the descendents and that given to Moses and Jesus and that given to all Prophets from their Lord; we make no difference between one and another of them (sura 2:136). Dispute ye not with the People of the Book [Christians] . . . but say, "We believe in the revelation which has come down to us and in that which has come down to you; our God and your God is One; and it is to Him we bow" (sura 29:46). Before this We wrote in the Psalms, after the Torah: "My servants, the righteous, shall inherit the earth" (sura 21:105). Say, "O People of the Book [Christians]! Ye have no ground to stand upon unless ye stand fast by the Turat [Torah], the Injil [Gospel], and all the revelation that has come to you from your Lord (sura 5:68).[4]

But what about the violence? This was the book of Islam, right, the "religion of hate"? Where were all the verses telling me to rise up and go slay the infidels?

They were there, all right, and they are quoted repeatedly these days, both by Muslim militants for purposes of exploitation and by their critics for purposes of denunciation. But I was wholly unprepared for how few and far between these verses are. In fact, when I listed all the verses embodying or advocating violence in the Old Testament and New Testament (at least, out of context), then tallied and compared these to a similar list drawn from the Qur'an, the Bible came out as three to five times *more* violent.

For example, here is one of the most infamous and often-quoted passages from the Qur'an's "verse of the sword":

> Slay the pagans wherever ye find them. And seize them, beleaguer them, and lie in wait for them in every stratagem. (sura 9:5)

Pretty stern stuff, especially if you're on the receiving end, as someone the Qur'an might consider a "pagan." But there are a few Old Testament verses I would be even more nervous about meeting in a dark alley:

> Now go and smite the Amalekites, and utterly destroy all that they have, and spare them not; but slay both men and women, young people and infants, oxen and sheep, camels and asses. (1 Sam. 15:3)

> You shall defeat them; then you shall utterly destroy them; you shall make no covenant [peace treaty] with them, nor show mercy to them. (Deut. 7:2)

And most poignant of all, the telegraphically brief commentary on what Joshua did upon conquering the little kingdom of Hazor:

> They . . . annihilated them, and they did not leave a soul among them. (Josh. 11:14)

"But there is a cultural and historical context for those verses," protest Christian apologists. "Sure, there are some six hundred passages of explicit violence in the Old Testament attributed directly to God—but they had their reasons! Those people were being persecuted by ungodly neighbors!"

Fair enough. But the same is true of the relatively fewer violent verses in the Qur'an. In A.D. 632, Muhammad and his followers signed a peace treaty with a neighboring tribe, the Quraysh. Two years later, the Quraysh betrayed the treaty and went on the attack against the Muslims' allies, the Khuzzas, nearly annihilating them. In fact, the term "pagans" in these suras does not refer to all people in the world who do not follow Islam; it refers specifically to the Muslims' military opponents of the time, who'd just abrogated a peace treaty and were massacring their friends.

Furthermore, even these verses are routinely distorted through selective quotation. Consider sura 9, *aya* 5, the commonly cited "violent verse" mentioned above:

> But when the forbidden [sacred] months are past, slay the pagans wherever ye find them. And seize them, beleaguer them, and lie in wait for them in every stratagem.

Sounds like a pretty unequivocal, unambiguous order for mass execution—until one realizes that those who quote it usually leave out the second half of the verse:

> But if they repent and establish regular prayers and practice regular charity, then open the way for them [let them go on their way]. For Allah is oft-forgiving, most merciful.

In fact, much like the ten commandments of the Tanach (Hebrew Bible), the Qur'an expressly forbids homicide:

> Take not life, which Allah hath made sacred, except by way of justice and law: thus doth He command you, that ye may learn wisdom. (sura 6:151)

If anyone slew a person—unless it be for murder or for
spreading mischief in the land—it would be as if he slew
the whole people; and if anyone saved a life, it would be as
if he saved the life of the whole people. (sura 5:32)

My purpose here is not to be an apologist for the Qur'an or a
critic of the Bible. It is simply to underline the extent to which I
had fallen prey to grave misstatements about the actual contents
of the holy book of Islam—and the extent to which I allowed
that misunderstanding to feed my passionately anti-Muslim
worldview.

I had believed that my own Bible told me, "Convert the hea-
then to the Christian religion." I had been flat wrong about that.
I had believed that the Qur'an told people, "Kill all the infidels,
namely, all those who don't follow Islam." I had been flat wrong
about that, too.

It soon became clear that if people on both sides of the growing East-West divide were to more fully grasp the true meaning
of the so-called violent verses in the Qur'an, it would contribute
immeasurably to the cause of peace—on two fronts. On the one
hand, it would nullify the arguments of the militants who use
these verses to recruit, promote, and instigate violence and terrorism. And on the other, it would reassure a suspicious and
threatened Western world inundated with terrifying misinfor-
mation claiming that the Qur'an—and by extension, the entire
civilization that professes to follow it—is inherently violent.

BUT THERE WAS still one major issue to wrestle with: where
did this so-called holy book come from, anyway? On whose authority did it say all these things? Who was this "Allah" that the
Qur'an kept referring to?

Throughout the Qur'an, I noticed, every single chapter but
one begins with these words: "In the name of Allah the Most

Gracious, the Most Merciful" (*Bayasmullah a-rahmanah a-rahim*). This sounded quite familiar. It seemed to echo, for example, the passage in Exodus wherein God appears to Moses to inscribe the ten commandments onto the two blank stone tablets the prophet carries, and God describes himself: "The Lord, the Lord, the God merciful and compassionate, long-suffering and abundant in goodness and truth" (Exod. 34:6).

Similar, yes, but was this a case of identity or imitation? Of unity or deception? Was this Allah the text kept referring to the same as the God of the Bible? The "one true God," the God of Abraham, Isaac, Ishmael, and Jacob? Or, as so many Christians seemed to believe, a false god? Is worshipping Allah really just a disguised version of corrupt idol worship?

My own belief from years past, that the Qur'an was the work of dark forces, was obviously predicated on the latter assumption. When I stormed out of that National Prayer Breakfast event in 1984 after hearing the Qur'an read to the assembly, it wasn't because I simply didn't care for what I'd heard—it was out of the fervent belief that it was a sinister and dangerous text, an utter corruption of faith and the product of an "Allah" that had nothing to do with the God I worshipped.

As it turns out, I was not alone in this belief. In 2003, Lt. Gen. William Boykin, the U.S. deputy undersecretary of defense for intelligence, made headlines by declaring that "Allah is not a real God" and that "Muslims worship an idol."[5] In 2005, Pat Robertson declared that the entire world was caught in a religious struggle over "whether Hubal the Moon God of Mecca, known as Allah, is supreme, or whether the Judeo-Christian Jehovah God of the Bible is Supreme."[6] A recent poll of Evangelical Christians asked if the participants believed that their God and Allah were one and the same; 6 percent said "yes," 2 percent weren't sure—and 92 percent said "absolutely not."[7]

Months of reading from sources of all sorts and persuasions soon made it clear that there were compelling arguments on all sides. But I had an advantage. I had a key: the Aramaic language.

Aramaic is not only considered the mother tongue of Hebrew, but it is also a very close cousin to Arabic. All three are Semitic languages, and in this simple but long-ignored fact lies tremendous hope for the future of our civilization.

The holy books of our modern monotheistic faiths are virtually impossible to compare in their modern versions, because they exist in *fundamentally incompatible languages*. Start with an English New Testament based on Greek or Latin, and an English Qur'an based on Arabic, and you're working with apples and oranges. But start from the Aramaic, and you are on common ground.

What did the Semitic languages have to say about God and Allah? The answer proved fascinating.

In pre-Muhammadan times, Arabs worshipped a moon god called Hubal, whom they also referred to as "Al-ilah," and this, goes the claim, was the source of "Allah." But *ilah* is simply the Arabic word for "god." *Al-ilah* means "the god." (The Arabic "al" is equivalent to the English "the.") In precisely the same generic way, Semitic tribes used this basic term, *il* or *el*, to refer to their various gods for thousands of years before Muhammad. El was the chief deity of the Canaanite pantheon; the Canaanite language was closely related to Hebrew. With Abraham and the birth of the great monotheistic faiths, these words were adopted to refer to the one God. The Aramaic form was *Alaha*, the Hebrew *Eloah*, which became the *Elohim* who does the creating in the first chapter of Genesis.

Taking a closer look at our own language, I found precisely the same linguistic process: our word "God" is derived from the proto-Germanic pagan word *gott*, which denotes a particular water spirit. The Latin *Deus*, from which we draw our word "deity," Spanish its *Dios*, and French its *Dieu*, are all descendants of *Zeus*, the name for the chief god in the Greek pantheon. Yet when modern Christians pray to God, Dios, or Dieu, we don't accuse them of invoking Zeus or a pagan water demon! The Hubal issue was a nonissue: *God, Dios, Elohim, Eloah, Alaha*—and yes, *Allah* as well—all refer to the same One Deity of Abrahamic monotheism.

For over five hundred years before the birth of Muhammad, Arab Christians and even some Jews in the Arabian peninsula used the word *Allah* for God. Roughly twenty million Arab Christians do so today. In fact, when Jesus spoke about God in everyday conversation, he would have used the same Aramaic word that every other Aramaic-speaker used: *Alaha*.

It seemed that the Recitation and the Testament were in agreement about many things indeed, including the God who had inspired their text. It was becoming extremely difficult to hang onto my staunch conviction that the Qur'an was anything but a genuine holy book to the Muslims, just as the Tanach is to the Jews and the New Testament to the Christians.

MY FORAY INTO the Reston bookstore had been well worth the emotional risk. At first, I had been curious, then intrigued; now I was thunderstruck. The crashing of my old paradigms now seemed quite complete: that comfortable, familiar righteous indignation that I had marshaled in response to the reading of the Qur'an at the National Prayer Breakfast in the winter of 1984 now lay in tatters.

But what bearing would this have on my professional life? I'd had what felt like an eye-opening revelation—but what could I actually *do* with it? The answer would not be long in coming.

FIVE

Miracle in the Sahara

In early April 1994 I was part of a citizen delegation that traveled to the Western Sahara to visit the indigenous Sahrawi people in their desert camps. The country had been torn by civil war for two decades, with the Sahrawi fighting against integration with Morocco, which they considered "the Occupiers."

Previously a Spanish colony (and sometimes known as the Spanish Sahara), the Western Sahara had been declared an independent nation by U.N. resolution in 1966. However, despite their nominal self-rule, the Sahrawi have been battling continuously for their independence ever since, first with Spain, then with Mauritania to the south and Morocco to the north, both of whom annexed huge portions of the land after Spain's withdrawal from the area. This desert, roughly the size of the state of Wyoming, is some of the most arid and uninhabitable land on the planet. Still, to the roughly 200,000 Sahrawi Muslims forcibly displaced from their ancestral land, it is home.

We landed in Algeria, bordering the Western Sahara's northeastern tip, where we were told to stay put and not venture into town. Radical Muslims were beheading people in the capital city of Algiers, we were told. We stayed put. Algerian president Abdelaziz Bouteflika had agreed to provide us with his personal plane to fly the final leg to the Sahrawi refugee camps, which lay just outside the Western Sahara within Algeria's borders. Like the Sahrawi people, Algeria was hostile to Morocco, and they were only too happy to help us. *The enemy of my enemy is my friend.*

We boarded the president's plane and headed south to the little city of Tindouf, which sits at the extreme western border of Algeria, jutting into the Western Sahara. After a while, the plane began to descend, and I fought the impulse to panic. There was no airport that we could see, no runways, no tower—just sand. Evidently the pilots knew something we didn't, because within the next few moments we touched down on what looked like a strip of pure sand blending almost imperceptibly into its sandy surroundings. It was the weirdest airplane landing I'd ever experienced.

I'd been to South Africa many times, but here, clear at the other end of the continent, it was a whole different story. Going to South Africa is a little like going to Sydney or London. This felt like a moon landing.

We deplaned, piled into a few four-wheel-drive vehicles, and headed out over the desert. Hours went by. Looking out toward the horizon, I could see absolutely nothing but sand. Waves of sand . . . an ocean of sand.

I asked our driver, "How do you know where the heck we are? Or where we're headed? Everything looks the same! It's like being on a raft in the middle of the ocean!"

He laughed and said, "Ah, we do this many times. We know where we're going."

We drove for an eternity that lasted about an hour, sometimes soaring up over sand moguls and slamming down into sand valleys, sometimes slaloming our way through sandy obstacle courses, mostly just plowing along the sandy straightaways. Finally, I saw a tiny dot on the horizon. The dot grew larger and larger, and then we had arrived.

Our destination appeared to be a tiny village composed of nothing but tents and a few buildings made of mud. Welcome to the Sahrawi refugee camp, I thought. Take us to your Hilton. We climbed out and followed our guide to our accommodations. Roberta McCain, Senator John McCain's mother, was part of our delegation. I marveled as she tromped through the sand like an eighteen-year-old. She was eighty-two. I was about half her age and already out of breath in the blistering heat.

AFTER WE'D GOTTEN settled, we were taken to a larger tent where we were to meet the exiled president of the Sahrawi Arab Democratic Republic (SADR) and secretary-general of the Polisario Front, the Sahrawi independence movement. We sat at a great banquet table, cross-legged on the tent floor, and waited.

Soon the great man strode into the tent. With deep scars on his face, he had the look of a man who had survived more than his share of fights—the serious kind. Muhammad Abdelaziz, soldier, warrior, leader of the Sahrawi people. Frankly, he looked terrifying. Since I was the head of the delegation, he strode directly over to where I was scrambling to my feet, smiled broadly, and reached out to shake my hand. And then we were sitting, talking and nodding as they brought us tea.

President Abdelaziz turned out to be extraordinarily friendly and warm, a genuinely charismatic leader. Once in conversation with him, you'd think you were talking with your favorite uncle. Your favorite uncle, that is, with deep facial scars.

Everyone was very cordial. Though Arabic is the official language of the Western Sahara, Spanish (of which everyone in our party had at least a modest command) is also spoken widely. We passed the time with diplomatic pleasantries and innocuous table talk. They brought in our dinner, and then, just as the food was set before us, Abdelaziz turned to me and said, "Tell me, Mark Siljander, why have you come? Exactly why are you here?"

The abrupt frankness of the question caught me completely off guard. Officially, we were a citizen delegation whose interest was peace and friendship—but what did that mean? We had no real mandate or effective power; there was nothing in particular we could offer. We were citizens, plain and simple. The real value of such trips generally boils down to whatever public relations mileage they might offer to either side.

Our "official" reason for visiting suddenly seemed wholly inadequate. Why *was* I here? What was I doing in the middle of the Sahara desert, sitting on a tent floor in 116-degree heat having tea with this man? I had a wife and four kids at home in a comfortable house in a D.C. suburb. Nobody was paying me to be here. What was I doing? Was I nuts?

All conversation had stopped; all eyes were on me, as everyone waited for my reply. I looked back at Abdelaziz. He knew that we had endured days of connecting flights and tiresome journeys through oceans of sand to be with him. Was there a reason, beyond the usual well-meaning but bland gestures of citizen diplomacy? I said the first thing that popped into my head—and it surprised me as much as I'm sure it did everyone else: *Al Kutbu al sharifa!* [The holy books!]

He raised his eyebrows, as if to say, *The holy books? Meaning what, Mark Siljander?* I don't know whether he was more surprised at what I said or at the fact that I said it in Arabic.

More words came tumbling out, although they were now Arabic mixed with Spanish (my Arabic was still far too basic to give voice to the complete thought).

"We're here to build bridges of friendship around the ideas of Isa that are in your Qur'an and also in our holy book."

His eyes opened wide. "You know the Qur'an?"

"I've just been reading it, yes, the last year or so."

"Tremendous!" he said.

"I think . . ." I wasn't sure just where this was going, but I couldn't stop now. "I think there are common links in our holy books, and . . ."—the thought had hardly formed when I heard myself articulating it here at this banquet table in the sand—

"and I think that if we can find those links and grow together in friendship, that we'll forge a path to peace and forgiveness, and you will achieve your struggle for independence from Morocco."

I didn't dare look at Mrs. McCain or the other members of our group, but I imagine there may have been a few gaping mouths. Muhammad Abdelaziz fastened his eyes on me for a moment without speaking. I couldn't read his reaction, and silently prayed that he would not feel grossly insulted. Then he said, "*El-hmdulellah!* [Thanks be to God]. Let's eat and discuss more."

WHAT HAPPENED NEXT seemed almost like a dream. We sat together and talked about the Qur'an and the Bible, about the teachings of Jesus/Isa and the real spirit of "submission" and "surrender" that was meant by the words later translated as "convert," about the linguistic unity of *Allah* and *Alaha* and *Elohim*, about the gulf of suspicion and misunderstanding between the civilizations of East and West.

And then, a little ways into our dinner, I surprised myself again by saying, "Look, I have a suggestion. Why don't you stop fighting the Moroccans?"

Just as it had before, all conversation at the table stopped. The warrior president looked at me and said, "How? What can we do? How would we go about doing this?"

"Why don't you just . . . stop?" I replied. "Instead of fighting, let's pray. Your people and my people believe in the same God, right? Let's pray. Tell you what, let's commit to pray together for the next six months. Our beliefs may be different, but they're not *so* different. We both believe in the power of the unseen world. We can pray together, whether it's through the Isa of the Qur'an or the Jesus of the Injil, or to God or Allah. And if nothing has happened after six months, then you can start fighting again, and I'll be the first one to support you."

He stared at me. I had no idea what he would do. Had I just put both feet in my mouth? I thought about my Aramaic teacher and mentor John Booko praying with Begin and Mubarak, and hoped I hadn't completely screwed up our visit.

Then he nodded thoughtfully and smiled. "All right," he said. "I'll do it."

The next day, Muhammad Abdelaziz stopped fighting and called for a cessation of all hostilities. He then went to Madrid, where he proposed an international conference of the parties most likely to form a joint monitoring commission for the Western Sahara, including Spain, France, Algeria, and Mauritania. On April 30 he wrote to the secretary-general of the United Nations, Boutros Boutros-Ghali, and suggested that the United Nations pursue this idea. In May, a meeting of experts convened at the Norwegian embassy in Washington to assess the feasibility of the plan. Among them was the former U.S. secretary of state, James A. Baker III, who became so involved in the issue that several years later he was appointed the United Nations' special envoy to the Western Sahara. The wheels of peace negotiations were suddenly turning—in high gear.

Years later, when I had the chance to meet with Jim Baker, I asked him, "What made you get involved in the Sahara? Of all the conflicts in the world, of all the possibilities for brokering peace, what in the world made you choose this relatively out-of-the-way place in the desert of western Africa?"

He thought about it for a moment, shrugged, and said, "To tell you the truth, I really don't know. I just felt compelled."

That fall, President Abdelaziz traveled to the United States and on his visit had the chance to sit down with me in a private meeting in Virginia. He shared what had transpired during the previous six months and shook his head, grinning from ear to ear.

"It is a miracle," he said, and I had to agree. "*El-hmdulellah!*"

The process, alas, did not hold. Within the ever-shifting agenda of American diplomatic priorities, there is little in the arid lands of the Western Sahara to grab and hold the spotlight for long. Between the fallout from our futile engagement in Somalia, which had culminated in the disastrous 1993 "Black Hawk down" incident in Mogadishu, and our intensifying engagement in Bosnia, Western Sahara got lost in the shuffle. Jim Baker kept trying for years, as did many other diplomats, and the effort continues to this day.

Despite the continual frustration of working toward resolution without success, my new friend's convictions held firm. Against considerable pressure from within the Polisario, Muhammad Abdelaziz has consistently resisted relaunching the armed struggle favored by many in the movement, insisting instead on a diplomatic and peaceful solution. He has become an outspoken critic of terrorism, sending formal personal notes of condolence to the governments of New York, Madrid, and London after the terrorist attacks in their respective cities. He even sent a similar note of sympathy to the Moroccan government—officially his sworn enemies—in the wake of the deadly al-Qaeda suicide attacks in Casablanca in 2003.

We had not effected a permanent resolution, but we had caught a glimpse of what was possible.

ACCORDING TO THE United States Institute of Peace, there are hundreds of peace and human rights organizations in the world right now working on over thirty-two peace treaties and initiatives, and twenty-five truth commissions working on a variety of organizational arrangements and recommendations. More than a dozen countries have commissions of inquiry or related bodies engaged in similar pursuit of strategies for peace and reconciliation, and there are hundreds of think tanks and religious efforts throughout the world working toward these same aims. We have had the United Nations as global arbiter and peace broker for more than half a century, and the world community has spent billions upon billions of dollars to design, enact, and enforce peace plans, supported by the might and power of the greatest armed forces in the world—and all have failed to address the basic elements of the conflicts they seek to address.

In 2005, King Abdullah II of Jordan convened a conference of Nobel laureates to discuss peace, security, and the fight against terrorism. Addressing the prestigious group, the king declared, "I look around this room and see a House of Wisdom—a global House of Wisdom for the twenty-first century and beyond."

Inspiring words, but the fact is, nothing really changed. The alienation continues to escalate at an alarming rate, and so does the violence. Why? Because despite the best of intentions, all such efforts continue to be predicated on the same approach—an approach that in and of itself cannot work.

When governments, institutions, or NGOs (nongovernmental organizations) set out to deal with a conflict, they invariably do so through combinations of the four established tracks of engagement: *diplomatic, political, economic,* and *military.* They dispatch *diplomats* to negotiate a resolution, use *politicians* and *political maneuvering* to implement those agreements, then apply carrot-and-stick pressure to the process with *economic incentives* or *sanctions* (carrots and sticks) and threats of *military retaliation* (the big stick). Hundreds of institutions of higher education have dedicated themselves to studying, developing, refining, and perfecting these traditional approaches to conflict resolution.

But there is a fatal flaw in this approach. No matter which tracks are used, in what combination or with what dedication and finesse, they don't strike at the heart of the matter. What is the heart of the matter? The *people* involved. Our *human nature.*

Even when negotiations appear to work, even when a given party agrees to accept certain terms of compromise with its enemies, their passions remain unchanged. If they hate their enemies before financial reparations, they will still hate them after the reparations. Forced gestures of goodwill don't change a thing. Whether they are bribed, convinced, coerced, or compelled, it is a contrived resolution, not a genuine one. Mechanical and external—not organic and internal.

This is not genuine conflict *resolution;* it is only conflict *containment.* And once the excitement and relief of the cease-fire, the temporary appeasement, the political and rhetorical accommodation wears off, the underlying conflict again rears its ugly head.

But there *is* a path to genuine, sustained peace and conflict resolution, and I had witnessed a whisper of it sitting on the floor of a tent in the Western Sahara, sharing views on the holy books with a battle-scarred Muslim warrior. The generosity of his friendship and the courage of his peace efforts in the ensuing months inspired me then, and they inspire me still today.

SIX

To Love Thine Enemies

One day in 1997 I was having lunch with Doug when a friend came by our table and said he wanted to introduce us to "someone from the Sudanese embassy." We both stood, and our friend made his introductions and then left the three of us to get acquainted.

Dr. Abubaker al-Shingieti occupied a position uniquely poised between two worlds. A longtime American resident, he not only had a diplomatic passport but also had a Green Card, owing to his marriage to an American citizen. He also traveled regularly to Sudan, which was one of the few countries in the world with which the United States had no diplomatic relations. In fact, he had an office in Khartoum, right across the hall from the president's, and continued to serve as a top presidential advisor in Sudan.

Conversation between the three of us soon turned to those issues of common ground that we had begun to explore since that trip to the Sahrawi refugee camp a few years before. As we related a few of my adventures in forging bonds with foreign leaders, Dr. al-Shingieti abruptly turned to me and said, "Why don't you come to Sudan and meet President al-Bashir?"

I have to admit, I paused before replying. Making such a trip would be quite a radical move. Sitting and talking about the holy books as part of a citizens' peace delegation to the Western Sahara was one thing. President Muhammad Abdelaziz was generally perceived as a pretty good guy and the leader of a people with a just cause.

Not so the president of Sudan. To say Omar Hassan Ahmad al-Bashir was not a popular man in the West would be the height of understatement. He had ruled his country with an iron grip ever since coming to power in a 1989 military coup. During those years, the country had been rocked by a bloody civil war, the largely Arab and Muslim north pitted against the mostly black and Christian or Animist (the majority, traditional African faith) south. Bashir's government had gained a reputation as one of the worst violators of human rights and religious freedoms in the world for hosting the likes of Carlos the Jackal and Osama bin Laden. There were reports of widespread violence against the Christian community, including torture of the clergy, destruction of churches and forced mass conversions, rape of the women, enslavement of the children, and ethnic cleansing.

I had visited many countries and met many Muslim leaders in the three years since that desert meeting with Muhammad Abdelaziz, but I had not sat down with a man the likes of Omar al-Bashir. I found myself wondering, had *anyone*? It occurred to me that, given Sudan's reputation, chances were good that there had been relatively few visits from any sort of U.S. delegations. I wondered aloud if this were the case.

Dr. al-Shingieti replied that, indeed, there had been relatively few such visits. In fact, there had been *none*. During all the long years of catastrophic conflict, he said, not a single U.S. official had gone to meet with al-Bashir or his people in Khartoum, whether officially, semiofficially, or even unofficially.

This seemed almost impossible to believe. "Not one?" I asked. "But I thought I'd heard ..." I was sure I'd seen something about someone going to Sudan, but I couldn't put my finger on who or when.

"Oh, plenty of congressmen and senators have been to Sudan," Dr. al-Shingieti assured me, "along with plenty of administration officials and other governmental and private-sector diplomats of all sorts. But every single one of them has gone only to the south, to meet with John Garang."

Ah, of course. John Garang was the leader of the Sudan People's Liberation Army, the so-called Christian rebellion against whom Bashir's forces were arrayed. Dr. al-Shingieti didn't need to explain further: Doug and I both understood. Why had all these dignitaries visited only the south? Because John Garang and his people were Christians. They were like us. They were not the "enemy."

And that, it now occurred to me, was perhaps the biggest flaw in our approach to foreign policy. Whether al-Bashir in Sudan or Kim Jong-il in North Korea (or today, Mahmoud Ahmadinejad in Iran), our diplomatic approach to our worst enemies is not much different from the common sulk response in a domestic feud: silence and a stubborn refusal to talk. *We don't want to appear weak,* as General Walters had said.

But if we won't talk, I thought, what hope is there of reconciliation? How can we possibly hope to reconcile two parties when we're only engaged in talking with one of those parties? Talking with our friends isn't difficult. But who's going to talk with the enemy?

It suddenly struck me how out of step we were with the holy books we professed to admire and whose teachings we claimed to emulate. Probably the most revolutionary thing Jesus ever said was that we should love our enemies unconditionally, even to the point of blessing them and praying for them.

But I say to you, Love your enemies, bless anyone who curses you, do good to anyone who hates you, and pray for those who carry you away by force and persecute you. (Matt. 5:44)

And it was not only the carpenter of Nazareth; the merchant of Mecca was just as familiar with the radical notion of reconciliation through forgiveness. By this time I had spent several years poring over the Qur'an, and knew that its text speaks of forgiveness more than 150 times.

> Remember Allah's favour on you: for ye were enemies and He joined your hearts in love, so that by His grace ye became brethren. (sura 3:103)

> Allah will grant love and friendship between you and those whom ye hold as enemies. For Allah has power; and Allah is oft-forgiving, most merciful. (sura 60:7)

The core of this radical teaching, as exemplified in both holy books, was that we love one another unconditionally—including our enemies. *Especially* our enemies.

Loving someone unconditionally simply means regarding and approaching him or her with genuine goodwill. When we think of our next-door neighbors or best friends, this doesn't seem much of a challenge. But what about neighbors in a civil war? What about someone who has caused pain and suffering for tens of thousands of innocent people? Omar al-Bashir was, in the eyes of the West, a bad man. In the eyes of God, as near as I could understand it, he was just another human being, with frailties and failings like the rest of us.

All of this whirled through my head as Dr. al-Shingieti sipped his coffee. How should we respond to this man's invitation?

A few years earlier, in 1994, Yitzhak Rabin and Shimon Peres were joint recipients of the Nobel Peace Prize for their work together that resulted in the Oslo Accords. There was a third recipient, too: their old nemesis—and mine—Yasser Arafat. Afterward, Rabin was harshly criticized for shaking the hand of Israel's archenemy during the Nobel prize ceremony. His reply

had engraved itself on my heart: "I make peace with my enemies, not my friends."

I looked at Dr. al-Shingieti and said the only thing I possibly
could. "Absolutely. We should go."

So Doug and I ponied up the funds together and went to
Khartoum.

SUDAN IS THE largest country in Africa, its more than forty
million people, two thousand tribes, and many religions spread
over a million square miles, an area as big as the entire eastern
half of the United States. Like so many European colonies
around the globe, Sudan achieved its independence in the years
following World War II (in this case, from Britain, in 1956). But,
as with so many European colonies after World War II, independence did not mean peace. Once the oppressive force of foreign
rule was gone, age-old internal divisions erupted into violence.

Even before independence was official, a full-fledged civil war
broke out that lasted seventeen years. A peace accord was
reached in 1972, but the peace was temporary. After a decade of
relative calm, civil war erupted again. It was still in furious full
force when Doug and I arrived.

The decades of war had wreaked economic havoc on this developing nation. During our visit, it was unbearably hot—rarely
falling below 100 degrees—and such amenities as working air
conditioning were few and far between. Arriving at the Khartoum airport, we were driven to the city's one decent hotel, a
Hilton—though this bore little resemblance to what we think of
as a Hilton in the West. After unpacking, showering, and settling
into our hotel room, we returned to the Hilton lobby to meet our
ride. Dr. Al-Shingieti met us in the lobby and accompanied us to
al-Bashir's home, an unimposing building near downtown
Khartoum, where we were met by aides and ushered into a
room. A few minutes later, the president entered.

Omar Hassan al-Bashir is not a tall man, but he is every bit as imposing a presence as was the warrior president I had met in the Western Sahara, very serious and *very* tough-looking. His formidable presence in every way lived up to his reputation as a fearsome autocrat. He wasted no time on pleasantries and got right down to asking us why we were there. (Though al-Bashir's English is quite good, he nonetheless used a translator; whether this was to effect a more intimidating impression, I couldn't tell.)

"We're not here in any official capacity," I explained.

I caught a glance flickering between Bashir and one of his aides, an expression I couldn't quite read. They knew very well that we were not an official delegation. They also knew that unofficially we represented the Prayer Breakfast Group, which comprised nearly one-fourth the members of the U.S. House of Representatives. Though we had no official capacity, there was clearly some force of authority behind our visit. And though that authority may have been more symbolic than actual, in international politics, symbolism goes a long way.

"We're here," Doug added, "as friends. We're not here to talk politics. We're here to—"

I heard a sharp *crack!* and just like that, the lights were dead. We were plunged into pitch darkness.

A WILD THOUGHT scrambled through my brain, one I had never had before and will most likely never have again: *Oh, my God, the Christians are about to kill us!*

Khartoum was not located near the fighting, which was mostly contained in the south. But still, this was a country at war—in fact, a country in its fifteenth straight year of war. Was it possible that John Garang's People's Front had penetrated as far north as the capital city? Were we under attack?

"Then tell me," the powerful bass voice floated out of the silky blackness, calmly and without a trace of concern, "what is your objective here?"

I could almost feel Doug's thoughts, and I was pretty sure they were the same as mine. *If the president's not worried, I guess we shouldn't be either.* Perhaps power outages were not uncommon in Khartoum. I cleared my throat and forged on.

"Our objective," I said into the darkness, "is peace for your people. And if we can contribute to that in any way, then *Insha Allah* [if God wills it]. But rest assured, we have no goal of trying to get you to do anything in particular. We have no political mission or—"

I heard a loud *whooossssh!* as somewhere in an unseen quarter of the building a generator kicked in—and the lights suddenly came on again, flickering with that peculiarly unstable light that says, *Hold on, we may go out again at any moment.* I blinked to clear my vision and realized that al-Bashir was gazing at me, waiting for the end of my sentence. I found my voice and continued.

"We have no political mission . . . and, other than forging the bonds of friendship, no particular agenda."

No particular agenda. Of course, I was not so naïve as to think that President al-Bashir himself had no agenda. Doug and I were meeting with an internationally despised despot, a man regarded by some as one of the world's worst terrorist sponsors and most ruthless dictators. For al-Bashir, our visit could potentially mean an extraordinary public relations coup: here's this man representing the U.S. Congress, and with him this influential elder statesman.

But I couldn't think about that. I didn't care what his intention was. If I really believed in what we were doing and the one whose name and teachings we were doing our feeble best to represent, then it didn't matter what al-Bashir thought or how he might think he was using us. We were here in pursuit of a bond that might put us all on a path toward peace. And that had to start with us.

"Actually," Doug chimed in, "we're here to pray with you."

For the first time, I saw a crack in al-Bashir's implacable demeanor. This was not something he had expected.

I took a breath and jumped on Doug's opening. "We're here because we know you are a devoted follower of the Qur'an, and we are also devoted followers of the same Allah and the same Isa that you know through the suras of the Recitation of the Prophet."

And with another *crack!* the lights blinked out again, plummeting us once more into the thick ink of complete darkness. I immediately wondered whether that last statement had been a mistake. We'd taken much the same tack as with Muhammad Abdelaziz in the Algerian desert—but al-Bashir was a very different person, and not an official "friend" but an official "enemy." Talking Jesus to the president of Sudan was a far riskier proposition.

In the disorientation of the utter darkness, the moment of silence felt like an eternity. I sensed that it was up to us this time to continue the conversation in the dark. I could almost feel al-Bashir challenging us with his silence: *Your turn, Americans. You were saying?*

Doug managed to pick up my thread. "We're here in the name of Isa, who taught us to love our neighbors as ourselves and to bless our enemies. We know that the north and south of your country have been enemies, but we also know that the Qur'an instructs us to follow Isa's teachings—"

And with a *whhooosh!* the power returned. I let out the breath I hadn't realized I was holding and glanced at al-Bashir. He opened his mouth slightly, as if to speak, but then stopped himself. Had Doug's comment angered him? Or just taken him by surprise?

For a split second I flashed back to the scene a decade earlier, when our nation's thirty-seventh president had told us Young Turks in the China Room of the Madison Hotel, "It's never a matter of trust—it's whatever serves our interests, that's what counts in the end." If it was genuine peace and reconciliation we were after, we needed to operate from precisely the opposite understanding:

It's not a matter of what serves our interests—it's a matter of building trust through friendship. That's *what counts in the end.* But how far could one extend such trust? Could we have the same conversation I'd had in the Saharan desert, with a man whom many considered one of the world's most oppressive leaders?

I spoke up.

"Of course, you can make peace with the south or not, sign a treaty or not, you do whatever you're inclined to do. But just know that we're going to be praying with you and for you in this process, and believing in you and in the very essence of what you call the power of Islam—being surrendered to God and in peace."

One of my greatest regrets in this life is that Doug and I did not have a photographer with us. If we had, a photo of President Omar al-Bashir's expression in that moment would grace the cover of this book. I've never seen anyone so overtaken by bafflement, so utterly at a loss for words. What was he going to say? "Sorry, I'm against peace"?

Our conversation went on for over an hour, and much to my amazement, it turned out after all to follow a course quite similar to that conversation with President Abdelaziz over the banquet table in a Saharan desert tent. We spoke about the Qur'an and the Injil, about Jesus and how he is regarded in Islam, about the true meaning of the Aramaic words usually translated as "convert" and why we didn't believe Jesus ever intended to create a "religion" or for people to be told to reject their culture and traditions, but only to surrender themselves to God. We did not speak about the war, about human rights, or anything remotely political.

When we returned to the United States, I reported our trip to my friends in Congress and the State Department. The State man gazed at me laconically. "Why the hell would you go to the north, Congressman?"

I smiled back. "Why wouldn't we?"

He looked like he was about to make a reply but then decided it wasn't worth it, that it would be like trying to talk to an idiot. He sighed. "All right, thanks for the report. That's all."

WHAT DID WE accomplish? Anything? In terms of the relationship between Sudan and the West, it's hard to say.

Our connection with President al-Bashir did not end with that lone visit. I knew that the link we'd created in Khartoum was tenuous and could easily crumble. That had been precisely the problem with developments in the Western Sahara: we weren't able to keep the connection going. After returning to the States, I got in touch with Dr. al-Shingieti and struck up a friendship that continues to this day (and about which I will say more presently). I have also stayed in contact with al-Bashir himself, visiting with him numerous times since then, both in other locations around the world and in Khartoum.

And there certainly was improvement on the diplomatic and political front. Within a few years, peace talks were under way in Sudan between the north and the south. The talks made substantial progress in 2003 and 2004, and on January 9, 2005, after two decades of continuous civil war, the peace was made official with the signing of the Naivasha Treaty, creating a unity government with a president and two vice-presidents, one to be a Christian from the south and the other a Muslim from the north.

Also, throughout the late nineties and into the new century, Sudan's position regarding terrorists and terrorism gradually moderated. Long regarded as a safe haven for global terrorists, Sudan reversed its position after the attacks of 9/11 and has since actively cooperated with the CIA in its fight against terrorism—a move that during the 1990s would have been even more unthinkable than a unity government in Sudan.

At the same time, Sudan remains one of the few nations not to have full diplomatic relations with the United States. And while the north-south civil war is long resolved, Darfur, Sudan's western region, has emerged as a major flash point of violence and a potentially serious threat to stability in the region, as well as the center of one of the worst human-rights tragedies of our era. As is all too typical of such conflicts, the Darfur situation has gotten completely mired in an international political stalemate, with various governmental parties—the United States, Britain, the United Nations on the one hand and Sudan on the other—entrenched in opposing positions about what steps will actually help resolve the crisis. In an effort to help maintain communication between the different factions involved, my friends and I have been in regular contact with Andrew Natsios, the U.S. special envoy to Sudan; Ali Karti, Sudan's state minister of foreign affairs; Ban Ki-moon, the recently appointed secretary-general of the United Nations; and President al-Bashir himself. As of this writing, it is still too early to say where these efforts will lead, but I remain hopeful.

Whatever direct impact our visit may or may not have had on the future of Sudan, one thing I can say for certain is that it was a watershed experience for me: it brought me face-to-face with a teaching that I had professed to follow for years and challenged me to embrace it, not as a nice Sunday school idea, but in actual practice, in direct confrontation with one of my country's worst enemies. In his first letter to the Corinthians, Paul wrote his famous paean to love:

> Love is long-suffering and kind; love does not envy; love . . . is not easily provoked, thinks no evil; rejoices not over iniquity, but rejoices in the truth; bears all things, believes all things, hopes all things, endures all things. (1 Cor. 13:4–7)

That is the love Jesus claimed was essential that we direct not only to our friends but also to our enemies.

There is one more thing I can say for certain about this trip and my many subsequent trips to Sudan: being in dialogue with al-Bashir and his friends has not always won me new friends here in the States. I've had people, including some in my own government, confront me accusingly, saying, "How can you sit at the same table with that man, knowing what's going on in his country, and just talk, like friends?"

To which I can only reply, "If it's really peace we're after, then how can we *not*?"

SEVEN

The Path of Ananias

During the years that followed, my friends and I began having many similar experiences in countries throughout Africa, the Mideast, the Balkans, Europe, and Asia. My experience in forging new friendships with foreign dignitaries and heads of state, especially in Muslim countries, was beginning to convince me that the teachings of Jesus offered a more reliable road map to East-West relations than the training I'd received in traditional politics and diplomacy.

Even more, these encounters continued to stretch me as a person, challenging me to confront my own beliefs and to put the strength of my convictions to the test. Nowhere was this testing process more difficult, more emotionally painful, and ultimately, more revealing than in our visit to the two largest Muslim countries in the world, Indonesia and Pakistan.

In late spring 2000, I traveled to Southeast Asia with Congressman Joseph Pitts, a Republican from Pennsylvania. Joe flew over a hundred combat missions during his three tours of Vietnam and knows firsthand the horrors of unresolved conflicts played out on an international scale. Since coming to Washington ten years ago, he has traveled extensively around the world as a leading advocate for human rights, especially in the context of religious persecution. Like a growing number of men and

women in our government and in the governments of dozens of
other nations, Joe has used his office to build relationships with
ambassadors and statesmen from countries all over the world in
an effort to create common ground and bridges toward peace
and reconciliation. Accompanying Joe and me were two people
who represented a Christian rights organization.

A Christian rights organization paying a call on two of the
world's largest Muslim populations—there could hardly have
been a more perfectly volatile context for exploring the possibility of bridges between the two worlds!

FIRST ON OUR agenda was a visit with Abdurrahman Wahid,
the president of Indonesia, which has the largest Muslim population of any country on the planet. I knew this meeting was
fraught with challenges. Indonesia had gone through a revolution in 1998 and was in the process of sorting out its democratic
processes, to put it mildly. (The country changed presidents four
times between 1998 and 2004.) In the midst of its political up-
heavals, the densely populated nation also became a hotbed of
rampant religious persecution and human rights abuses.

The little delegation of two Christian leaders was intent on
addressing these issues head on. The more I thought about it,
the more uneasy I grew with this approach; I suspected that this
was a strategy far more likely to fail than a softer, less confronta-
tional approach.

Before our meeting with the president, we sat down to talk
about the dilemma that faced us. The last thing our hosts wanted
to hear was another Western Christian organization telling them
what was wrong with the way their country was being run. But
what could we do? We couldn't simply ignore these issues; they
sorely needed addressing.

As we talked, my thoughts turned to a passage in the New
Testament.

"Hey," I said, thinking out loud, "let's look for a moment at what Jesus said to Ananias in Damascus."

As recorded in Acts, Jesus appeared in a vision to this man and gave him instructions for Saul of Tarsus, the famous persecutor of Jesus's followers who would soon have a massive change of heart and eventually become the apostle Paul.

"He said Saul was a chosen vessel, right?" I continued, "a vessel meant to carry Jesus's name to Jews, Gentiles, and kings."

"Are you saying," one of our group began dubiously, "that we're supposed to carry Jesus's name to President Wahid? I'm not sure how well *that's* going to go."

Actually, Jesus's name was already quite well known to devout Muslims everywhere—but that wasn't what I was getting at here.

"No, my point is that Saul wasn't commissioned to *convert* the kings or to bring any sort of religious system or specific set of policies. He was told simply to 'carry his name.' In other words, just go in peace and friendship, in the name of Jesus, to be representatives of his teachings. To offer goodwill and unconditional love, and even bless and pray for our enemies. Let these other issues come up naturally, as God wills it."

Nobody said anything, but I could see what my friends were thinking. I was thinking the same thing myself.

"I know," I said, "this seems totally contrary to logic. Honestly, the entire Sermon on the Mount is contrary to human logic! But that's what he taught. And you have to admit," I added, "as role models for successful diplomacy go, Saul of Tarsus is not bad. He turned practically the whole world upside down."

Even so, none of us was entirely convinced. It seemed like a good and noble idea, in theory—how could one do better than follow Paul's example? But still, there were these horrendous human rights issues that badly needed to be addressed, and they obviously weren't going to address themselves. It seemed like an intractable dilemma. In the end, what we did was pursue not one course or the other, but both together—and we failed miserably.

When we met with President Wahid, we talked about Jesus/ Isa and discussed some of his teachings and how they represented a bridge between our different cultures and faith traditions—and we also broached the topic of religious rights for Indonesian Christians and some of the more heinous human rights abuses that were going on within his country's borders. The presentation was diluted and confusing. President Wahid interpreted the visit as a "religious mission." The meeting was an unmitigated disaster, and as far I could see, nothing of any substance came out of it.

THAT NIGHT, I thought some more about that passage from Acts. If, I thought, we are called, like Paul, to "carry the name of Jesus," just what does that mean? Jesus is commonly referred to in the New Testament (as in common speech today) as Jesus the Christ or simply Jesus Christ. Jesus is the man's name; what does the title "Christ" mean? I cannot count the number of times I have put this question to Muslims and Christians alike and gotten back a puzzled "I don't really know" in response.

In fact, *christ* or *kristos* is simply the Greek translation of the term "messiah." Which brings us one step closer to real meaning, but not the whole way: most people think of "messiah" as having some vague connotation having to do with "savior" but don't know what the word truly *means*.

The word "messiah" is derived from the Aramaic word *mesa*, meaning "oil." In the hot, dry climate of the Middle East, the precious richness of *mesa* held great value, both as cash and as symbol. Political leaders, such as kings, priests, and some prophets, were anointed with oil—typically with oil being poured over the head—before taking office.[1]

"Messiah" means one who is anointed with oil. In the tradition of the Torah, anointing with oil was considered sacred and reserved for the most holy. For example, Moses was instructed to make such anointing oil for Aaron to become a priest (Exod. 30:22–37), and in other passages, kings, prophets, and priests were anointed with oil, symbolizing the Holy Spirit (Isa. 61:1, Zech. 4:1–6).

The Torah prophesies *forty-seven* times of the coming messiah who would be anointed with spirit by God (Aramaic: *Alaha*) to serve in all three positions: prophet, king, and priest.

The New Testament identifies Jesus as this messiah (hence the Greek *kristos*, or Christ), starting in the very first chapter of Matthew: "Mary, of whom was born Jesus, who is called Christ" (Matt. 1:16).

And so—as most in the West are shocked to learn—does the Qur'an, in precisely the same manner: "His name will be Masih, Isa" (sura 3:45). In fact, the Qur'an describes Isa as *masih* (Arabic for "messiah") in this same way *eleven* times, and nowhere applies this term to any other prophet than Isa.

Both faiths agree that Jesus was a prophet, and even that he was king of the kingdom of heaven within our hearts. But what of the priestly duty of messiah? The traditional Semitic priestly duties included the slaying of a pure, spotless lamb as an intermediary for the remission or compensation of our sins. Muslims even today perform this traditional ceremony during the pilgrimage of hajj. In the Qur'an, Jesus was also called a "mediator" (*wajih*) and "intercessor" (*shafa'a*), which would certainly seem to evoke exactly this priestly function.

Isa the Masih, prophet of the Injil and Qur'an alike, our mediator and intercessor . . .

With a sigh my thoughts returned to the meeting earlier that day. We had not been very effective at carrying the name of Jesus the Priest and Mediator. We had tried to be mediators and intercessors ourselves, standing in for the rights of the oppressed and downtrodden of Indonesia, and we had done a poor job of it.

We left the country the next day feeling discouraged and defeated.

FROM INDONESIA WE traveled on to Pakistan, the world's second most populous Muslim country, where our group was to meet with the country's chief executive and head of state, General Pervez Musharraf. General Musharraf had just assumed power through a bloodless coup d'état the previous fall (a year later, in June 2001, Musharraf would formally assume the office of president), and just as in Indonesia, the country was going through some adjustment. Also, just as in Indonesia, there were grievous human rights issues that our group was keen on addressing, especially the mistreatment and persecution of Pakistani Christians.

Upon our arrival at our hotel in Islamabad, we were scheduled to meet with a group of Christian Pakistani women whose husbands had been imprisoned under sharia (Islamic law) on frivolous or trumped-up charges. Because it was next to impossible for women in this society to find work that could support their families, the men's prison terms were just long enough to force many of these families literally into starvation. Thus, though the sentences for the incarcerated men could be portrayed to the world as mild, they were tantamount to death sentences for the families left behind.

We found our way to the room that had been set aside for this meeting. There, waiting for us, were twenty-two Pakistani women, with at least as many children clutched to their waists and clinging to their ankles. They had all obviously dressed in the best clothing they had, such as it was; many of them were just as obviously on the edge of poverty already.

"Thank you for agreeing to see us," began the young woman who had accompanied them and served as their translator. (None of us spoke Urdu, the official tongue of Pakistan, and none of the twenty-two women spoke anything but Urdu.) "We are so grateful you are here. . . . There is no one else."

The English was a little clumsy, but the meaning was clear: *There is nobody else who can help us. You're our only hope.* Even if there had been no one present to speak in English, the desperation in their eyes, women and children alike, spoke more eloquently than any words possibly could.

As heartbreaking as this was, the meeting we held among ourselves afterward was even more difficult. We huddled in our hotel rooms, emotionally drained from our encounter with these broken and pleading families, and began to talk about what approach we ought to take in our forthcoming meeting with General Musharraf. It was one of the most difficult meetings of my life.

In Indonesia, there had been people suffering who had nobody to represent them, people with families, people who had hurt no one and were being persecuted for reasons completely outside of their control. Here in Pakistan, not only was this true but we had also just sat with them, seen them with our own eyes, heard their voices and felt their tears.

What could we do? We were all absolutely clear that we simply *had* to bring up the issue of these twenty-two women and their families. Yet our experience told us that this was precisely what we could *not* do. I was the one who gave voice to this awful thought.

"I just don't think it's a good idea," I said. "I don't think we can bring it up."

The others stared at me as if I were the most coldhearted person in the world.

"I know, I know," I said miserably. "Of course we all ache for these sweet, wretched people who are so innocent of any crime and are being treated so badly. How could our hearts not be breaking right now? But we have to remember that behind these twenty-two families, there are twenty-two *hundred* more that we have yet to meet. And behind them, twenty-two *thousand*."

With this image I succeeded only in making us feel still more hopeless. How many suffering people were there in the world—and what could individual people like us possibly do to help ameliorate their torment?

"So, what are you suggesting?" said one of our friends. "That it's like a catch-22? If we try to talk about it, we risk offending him and getting nowhere—but if we don't try, then we've accomplished nothing!"

She had a point. What *was* I suggesting, exactly? I thought again of Ananias.

"Saul was sent out to talk to kings. Well, we're only going to have one chance with this particular 'king.' It seems to me, we have two choices. We could try to exercise the power of what we can see and touch, and throw our agenda down before him in the manner of a demand. Or we could throw our lot in with the unseen and do as Ananias was instructed, as Jesus taught in the beatitudes when he said, 'Blessed are the peacemakers' and 'Love your enemies.' We could go before Musharraf in a mission of pure goodwill and unconditional love . . ."

"And let God set the rest of the program," Joe completed the. thought.

We all sat in silence. I don't know whether it was that we were simply desperate or that our painfully disappointing experience in Indonesia had made us more receptive to trying something different. Or perhaps the emotional exhaustion that followed our wrenching meeting with the Pakistani women had simply made us all more vulnerable, and therefore more open to new ideas. Whatever the reason, this time the idea of actually setting our feet on the path of Ananias seemed, if no less crazy an idea, at least something worth trying. What else was there?

I spoke up once more. "We could go with pushing our agenda, or we could go with Ananias's agenda. And honestly, which strategy do we think will give these twenty-two women and their kids a better chance of a successful outcome?"

We decided to try it Ananias's way.

THE NEXT DAY we met with Musharraf. When he asked us what was the purpose of our visit, Joe told him that we had no agenda; we had come from America to see his country and simply wanted to be his friends.

"You want to be my friends," Musharraf repeated, as if he weren't sure he had understood us correctly. (Urdu is not a language I've yet managed; we conducted the entire audience in English.)

Joe nodded. "Yes, in the spirit of Isa of the Qur'an."

Musharraf visibly blanched. "You know the Qur'an?"

I chimed in. "Yes, your Excellency, and there are quite a few of us who meet regularly to study your holy book along with ours, and we've been quite amazed to find so many similarities and correspondences between the two."

By this time I felt fairly solid about this approach. My friends and I had talked with Muhammad Abdelaziz and Omar al-Bashir and many other Muslim leaders and dignitaries in many other countries, and the consistency and similarities of their responses had gone way beyond the confines of fluke, coincidence, or luck.

Sure enough, General Musharraf's entire posture changed. The defiance and military bearing seemed to evaporate from him like a wraith, and he leaned forward, at once relaxed and intrigued. "Really. Who is this who meets like this?"

We talked with him about the congressional prayer groups we had formed, where we leave politics at the door for one hour each week and meet to discuss issues of friendship, colloquy, and collaboration on projects we feel could be better accomplished as friends than as political allies. We invited him to be part of this network of friends. At first, I am quite sure he believed that our invitation was not genuine but rather a formality of diplomatic politesse. But we repeated the offer, and affirmed that we meant it.

At this point, our two friends from the human rights organization began passing notes to Joe, urging that he bring up the issue of the husbands of the twenty-two women and ask for their release. "It's going so well!" they scribbled. "Now's the time to ask!"

Were they right? We certainly seemed to have achieved a strikingly congenial atmosphere; one would be hard-pressed to imagine an ambience more conducive to amiable negotiation. It did indeed seem the perfect moment to press our advantage and ask for what we wanted.

Yet I couldn't do it. Something stopped me. It was that phrase that I had felt enter my thoughts: *To press our advantage. To win him over to our way of thinking.* Was that any different, really, than saying, "to convert him"? As noble and urgent as our goal felt to me, wouldn't giving in to the temptation to press our advantage, in that moment, somehow violate the very spirit of the enterprise?

I glanced over at Joe, and silently prayed that he would stick to his guns and not veer off the path of Ananias. He did. Hasty note-passing notwithstanding, the issue of the twenty-two suffering families was not raised, not a word, during the entire time we were there. Not, that is, until the very end of our meeting—and it was not raised by us.

After nearly an hour had passed in convivial and fascinating conversation, we all prayed together—I've noticed in my time with Muslims that they tend to pray a good deal more than Christians do—and then stood to leave. The chief executive of Pakistan motioned us to be seated again.

"Wait," he said. We sat. "I know that you have some concerns, about some men who have been incarcerated under sharia law." He stopped. The four of us sat frozen. Musharraf continued. "Twenty-two men, I understand."

And now Joe decided to go for broke. It was Musharraf who had brought the subject up, after all, and not us. That made it fair game, it seemed to Joe, and at this point I was having the exact same thought.

"Yes, your Excellency," Joe replied. "In fact, we did have the opportunity to meet with the wives of these men."

We went on and shared our concerns, without recrimination or condemnation, just speaking our truth, as one would with a friend. The country's head of state listened and nodded, noncommittal but open. After that, our audience was over. We returned to our hotel and soon thereafter departed for the States. Several weeks after our visit, the twenty-two men were released.

I have never forgotten the faces of those twenty-two women.

My Apology

I should start by saying that I never did come face-to-face with Muammar Qaddafi, although that had been the plan. Libya's infamous head of state changed his mind at the last minute, so our meeting ended up being with Qaddafi's foreign minister instead—but that was far from the biggest surprise of the whole episode.

During the Reagan years, Colonel Qaddafi was the ultimate bad actor on the global scene.[1] To the West of the 1980s and early 1990s, he was Saddam Hussein and Osama bin Laden wrapped into a single package.

Actually, even this doesn't quite spell it out in full. In an era when we were shifting our focus from communism to Muslim extremism as global foe number one, Qaddafi embodied not one or the other of these forces but *both*. He even coined a term for his communistic approach to Arab nationalism: "Islamic socialism." He believed passionately in the unification of all Arab states into one pan-Arab nation, and tried in the early 1970s to forge Libya, Egypt, and Syria into a Federation of Arab Republics.

Qaddafi became a strong supporter of Arafat's Palestine Liberation Organization, which only deepened his worsening reputation in the West. In fact, he had a policy of supporting liberation movements—and to the bafflement of us in the West, he would throw his support behind even those resistance movements whose aims and ideologies he himself disagreed with. By the mid-1980s, he was widely considered in the West to be the principal sponsor of international terrorism.

The West's antipathy for Qaddafi reached its peak during the years I was in office. In 1982 the Reagan administration imposed economic sanctions and banned the export of U.S. oil technology to Libya. In 1986 the United States clashed with Libya in the disputed waters of the Gulf of Sidra and attacked Libyan patrol boats in multiple sorties, soon followed by bombing raids over Tripoli and Benghazi, in retaliation for Libya's involvement in the deadly bombing of a German nightclub known to be frequented by Americans. Among the dozens of Libyans killed in the bombing raids was Qaddafi's adopted daughter, Hanna.

Two years later, in December 1988, Pan Am flight 103 was downed over Lockerbie, Scotland. Its wreckage crashed into the little town of Sherwood Crescent, killing eleven townspeople in addition to the 259 victims on the plane itself, 189 of whom were Americans. It was the worst act of terrorism against U.S. civilians in history and would remain so until the disastrous attacks of September 11, 2001. The investigation (the largest in Scotland's history) soon found evidence of a bomb planted aboard the airliner, and two members of Libyan intelligence were charged with planting the device.

But despite world outcry, Qaddafi refused to extradite the two men. As a result, Libya endured harsh economic sanctions and diplomatic isolation throughout most of the 1990s. From the United States, in particular, the isolation was absolute: there was no trade with Libya, no diplomatic relations, no talks, nothing. American citizens couldn't visit Libya even if they wanted to—which nobody did. For us, it was as if Libya no longer existed.

However, my friends and I had a rather unusual connection. We had struck up a friendship with Qaddafi's neighbor to the south, Mathieu Kérékou, the president of Benin.

IN 1997, NOT long after that first trip to Sudan, I traveled with my friend Jim Inhofe to a number of African countries, including Togo, Côte d'Ivoire, and Nigeria—all of them at the time run by ruthless dictators. In the midst of that trip, we had spent several days in Benin with its remarkable president. Mathieu Kérékou had been a committed Marxist-Leninist dictator for nearly two decades but had denounced Marxism in 1990 when he became the first African dictator to institute a democratic government in his own country. In fact, he was so committed to having his country run by a genuinely free democratic system that the following year, when he failed to achieve the majority vote in Benin's first multiparty election, he stepped down and waited five years until he could run again. (He was reelected president in 1996 and again in 2001, then stepped down yet again in 2006 because Benin's constitution did not allow a third consecutive term.)

A few years before our visit, President Kérékou had gone through a profound change of heart and had become committed to the teachings of Jesus. While the U.S. State Department argued strenuously that this was nothing but a false front put up by yet another despotic African leader, it was clear to us that his transformation was genuine.

Over the course of our two days there, Jim and I spent a good fourteen hours with President Kérékou and his wife in their home in Cotonou, the capital of Benin. The little house was nothing fancy, especially for a head of state (the place was barely cooled by an aging air conditioner humming along in one window), but we felt curiously at home.

Benin has a very diverse population, ethnically, culturally, and linguistically. While both Islam and Christianity are well represented, there is also still a strong presence of the indigenous belief called Vodun, which is believed to have been the origin of voodoo. Not too long ago, Mathieu told us, there had been a good deal of fighting among the different ethnic and cultural groups. Inspired by the teachings of Jesus and wanting to bring peace to his country, he set in motion an extraordinary chain reaction of reconciliation.

He started by establishing a Youth Corps composed of the poorest of the poor. These kids began to learn trades so they could support themselves and, at the same time, to learn about Jesus—not Christianity per se, just the teachings and spirit of Jesus. Soon these youths began traveling from village to village. When they came to a new location, the locals would ask them who their chief was. They would simply reply, "Well, you wouldn't know him." After a while the villagers insisted on knowing the identity of these mysterious children's chief, and the kids would say, "Well, it's this man Jesus." Before long, several dozen villages had become followers of the teachings of "this man Jesus" and these ideas of love, forgiveness, and reconciliation. Now, our host told us as he beamed with pride about these young goodwill ambassadors, there were thousands of children throughout the country plying their trades and spreading their chief's ideas.

As of this writing, Benin is one of only four countries in all of North Africa rated "free" by Freedom House, a D.C.-based NGO that issues annual reports on civil and political rights in every country of the world.[2] (So much for State's assessment of the sincerity of the man's change of character.)

At one point in our wide-ranging conversation, President Kérékou said to us, "You know, in your country you have an expression, 'What would Jesus do?' I like this. I would like to run my country the way Jesus would, if he were running it. But I have no idea exactly how to do that." He looked at Jim and then at me with an expression of disarming candor. "Do you have any suggestions for me?"

This time it was my friend Jim's face that I wished I could capture on camera. It's not every day a head of state asks you for advice on how to run his country.

"Mr. President," I began, "it sounds like you're doing an amazing job already. I really don't see what we could add. But I would say this: since there are so many different religious expressions in Benin, *don't start calling yourself a Christian.* There's no need to pigeonhole yourself. Once you're labeled a Christian, all kinds of people start having all kinds of expectations and views—both good and bad—about what you're doing, based purely on the label. Just keep following what Jesus taught—and don't call yourself anything but a *follower of Jesus.*

"Jesus said to love your neighbors as yourself, and to love and bless your enemies. And he said, 'Blessed are the peacemakers, for they shall be called sons of God.'

"Actually, Mr. President, from what I can see, I think you have a pretty good sense of exactly what Jesus would do."

PRESIDENT KÉRÉKOU WAS now a staunch advocate of a free, democratic state; however, for the two decades before that, he had been just as dedicated a Marxist-Leninist, ruling Benin with all the autocratic gusto of a Tito or a Mao. He knew Castro, Saddam, Arafat, all the revolutionaries and radicals and freedom fighters. As we would put it in Beltway-speak, the man had quite a Rolodex. And among his circle of good friends, naturally, was Colonel Qaddafi.

Now, in early 1999, President Kérékou got word to me that he had set up a meeting between myself and Libya's leader. "I told the Colonel he needs to sit down and talk with you, Mark," said my friend, and that was that. I agreed to go, and invited Doug to come with me.

This would be the most difficult trip to pull off of any we'd ever taken, in a strictly logistic sense. It would also be the most dangerous. Because strict U.S. sanctions were in place, we couldn't legally travel to Libya using U.S. passports. We couldn't secure visas or plane tickets for Libya. And if we somehow managed to get into the country, we would be constrained by U.S. law from spending any currency. Buying a slice of bread or a taxi ride would be a criminal act.

With Mathieu's help, we were able to surmount all these hurdles by concocting a plan that felt a bit like the setup for an elaborate heist, yet was (according to all the advice we could muster) technically legal. First, we would fly from D.C. to Paris, then from Paris to Cotonou. Meanwhile, Colonel Qaddafi would send his own private jet to the Cotonou Cadjenou Airport to pick us up in the dead of night, when nobody would see us. Using the colonel's jet, the four of us—Doug and myself, Mathieu, and Romain Zannou, a trusted advisor of Mathieu's whom I had met on that earlier visit to Benin—would then fly to Tripoli. Doug and I would leave our passports and all I.D. behind in Benin. Nobody else would know we were going, except for our wives and a few heads of state. For a few days, essentially, we would not exist.

As the plan took shape, Doug and I and our wives briefly debated the wisdom of the whole idea, weighing merits against safety. But it was a perfunctory exercise—we all knew we were going. There was no way we were going to pass up an opportunity like this.

Toward the end of March 1999, our bags were packed and we were about to leave for Paris—when I got a frantic call from President Kérékou.

"My friend, I don't think I can go to Tripoli," he said, his voice thick with emotion.

I was aghast. "Why? Mathieu, what happened?"

"Your ambassador got wind of our plans," he began, and I sank back into my chair. I had a pretty good idea as to what was coming next.

It has been my experience that the U.S. Department of State, like most foreign ministries, universally rejects the idea of building personal relationships as a means toward reconciliation. Even when viewed as supplemental to the more conventional approaches of diplomatic, political, economic, and military engagement, gestures toward personal friendship are seen as signs of weakness, at times even a serious threat to potential negotiating positions.

This isn't summer camp, Ambassador Siljander, it's global diplomacy. We don't want to appear weak.

On countless occasions when I have been engaged in overseas missions, attempting to pursue friendships with foreign dignitaries, the U.S. embassy has been more obstructionist than supportive. In public, diplomats and foreign ministers often give lip service to the value of heart-to-heart meetings and person-to-person diplomacy, and speak in glowing terms of the new friendships between their presidents and prime ministers or other heads of state. In the privacy of their confidential conversations and strategy meetings, such relational issues are given a priority of zero, if not actually quantified with a negative number.

I sighed inwardly. "What did he say, Mathieu?"

"Well, I suppose you can guess. 'We have been making great progress together, the United States and Benin,' he said, 'and we're concerned that you may be jeopardizing all of that.'" He paused, and I could feel how painful this was for him. "I'm sorry, Mark. I don't think I can go."

"No, of course you can't," I replied. "But what are the chances that *we* can still keep our appointment?"

His voice brightened a bit. "Well, if you and your friend are still willing to go, I can still send Romain to accompany you."

"How will that be perceived on their end?" I asked, already knowing the answer.

"I have no doubt that Colonel Qaddafi will take this as a slight and be offended. But if you want to go, we'll provide all the arrangements, just as planned."

It angered me that State had muscled my friend this way, and it annoyed me that they had done an end run, calling him on the eve of our trip rather than coming and speaking directly to me. But I was determined to salvage our mission if at all possible. I told President Kérékou the plan was a go; Doug and I left for Cotonou, by way of Paris, the following morning.

Colonel Qaddafi was not only offended, he was furious. Livid. He saw our delegation as a flagrant bait-and-switch—which, truthfully, is exactly what it was, though not by our intention—and as Mathieu and I had both feared might happen, he refused to see us. If our head of state would not deign to keep the appointment, why should theirs? If we were coming only with Benin's foreign minister, then it would be Dr. Omar al-Montasser, Libya's foreign minister, who would meet with us, and not the colonel himself. It was a bad footing to start on, but at least we were seeing someone very highly placed in the colonel's inner circle.

In Benin, at the appointed hour, the colonel's private plane arrived on the tarmac at Cotonou Cadjenou Airport. The markings on the jet's exterior (in English and Arabic) said "ambulance"—but the only medicinal thing on board was the cognac. Under the cloak of night the three of us flew, one of us with passport and two of us without, to keep our date in Tripoli.

The meeting in Libya began on a difficult note. Dr. al-Montasser ignored Rev. Zannou and raged at the two of us Americans. He said he knew we were there to heckle him about the Lockerbie suspects and he wasn't interested in talking about it. We told him that was not our intention. Yes it was, he insisted, and he launched into another tirade.

A second time, we denied having this agenda, and a third time he lit into us about it. We had lied about coming with President Kérékou, and now we were lying about the purpose of our mission.

"Our countries are the worst of enemies, yours and mine," al-Montasser bellowed, "and this is why: you are all liars who lie about everything!"

"Our countries may be enemies," I ventured, "but those of us in this room are not enemies. We have never met you before, and we are here right now with only one purpose."

He glared at me and waited for me to go on, ready to pounce on whatever foolish lie I might next try to put across.

"Our entire objective here is friendship. That's all. We're here to pursue a new relationship, based on the teachings of Isa—"

That was it. I might as well have tossed a stick of dynamite into his lap. Dr. al-Montasser leapt to his feet and started screaming at us.

"What do you think, we're all Christians here?! What kind of American arrogance do you think—"

"I'm sorry if I've offended you," I interjected, "but Christianity doesn't have 100 percent ownership of Jesus—I was referring to Isa al-Masih, the Isa of the Qur'an."

"The Qur'an?" he yelled at me. "What do you Christian Americans know of the Qur'an?"

When I'd visited Togo and Nigeria with Jim Inhofe, I'd had a moment of genuine terror. Togo's president, Gnassingbé Eyadéma, who was then the longest-running African president in modern history, was the absolute stereotype of the ruthless African dictator, maintaining his autocratic rule (and absurdly luxurious lifestyle) through sheer force. He was said to be quite free with torture; according to rumors, he had some of his opponents fed alive to crocodiles. Not your friendliest head of state. A few days later, when Jim and I met with Sani Abacha, the unspeakably corrupt ruler of Nigeria, there was a moment when

Abacha sent all his aides out of the room and I wondered if I was ever going to see Nancy and my four kids again, or if we were going to end up in a Nigerian lake—if Abacha had borrowed a few of Gnassingbé Eyadéma's crocodiles to eat the annoying Americans.

This was worse. Nobody officially knew we were there. We had no passports; we had not flown a commercial flight. We could disappear pretty easily here—as others actually have—and here was Qaddafi's right-hand man, inches from my face, screaming at me, demanding to know what I thought I knew about the Qur'an.

Despite the intensity, even the urgency, of the situation, his challenge struck me to the core. Time slowed down, and I found myself momentarily lost in self-reflection.

What *did* I really know? I had professed to be carrying a message of reconciliation. But how genuine was this? I certainly was sincere about wanting to offer our friendship—but out of what motives? With what state of mind? With all my talk about Jesus and love, did I still secretly harbor the thought that my friends and I were morally superior to this man standing before me? That Qaddafi and his henchmen were the bad guys, and we the good guys? Was I standing in judgment, driven still by a remnant of that old, deeply ingrained impulse to go for the "conversion"?

I thought about Tony Hall.

TONY WAS A Democrat from Dayton, Ohio, who had served in the U.S. House of Representatives for nearly twenty years and would continue in that seat until 2002, when President George W. Bush nominated him to succeed George McGovern as U.S. ambassador to the U.N. Agencies for Food and Agriculture. Tony has focused throughout his career on the scourge of world hunger. He was founder of the Congressional Friends of Human

Rights Monitors and the Congressional Hunger Center. In 1993, when his Select Committee on Hunger was abolished, Tony protested by fasting for twenty-two days.

Tony was also a man of great spiritual values, one who professed to follow the teachings of the carpenter from Nazareth, and he had inspired me with what seemed to me a radical act that exemplified the teachings of Jesus in the Sermon on the Mount. In the search for reconciliation on a massive scale, he had apologized from the floor of Congress—to the United States and the world at large—for crimes committed by the institution and perpetuation of slavery.

I don't mean he apologized as a proxy, offering an abstraction of contrition on behalf of states, countries, and ancestors long since passed from the face of the earth. He apologized *personally*.

A few years earlier, while researching the history of slavery in America, Tony discovered something that shook him: there had never been any kind of formal apology for the crime of the American slave trade.

"Mark," he had said to me, "it's just unconscionable. This isn't some abstract event in history we can forget and put behind us. And it isn't something we can lay at someone else's feet. *We* have to address this."

The issue became a burr in Tony's side. It simply wouldn't let him rest. In 1997 he introduced a resolution to the U.S. Congress formally apologizing for the institution and wretched history of slavery in America. Though his bill never made it out of committee, it generated quite a public stir.

For some reason, as I sat in this clandestine meeting in a government office in Qaddafi's Tripoli, Tony's words came back to me: *This isn't something we can lay at someone else's feet.*

Dr. al-Montasser's bulldog face was still inches from mine, his bellowed challenge echoing in the air about us.

What do you Christian Americans know about the Qur'an?

"Surely not all I should," I said, doing my best to convey a calm I did not feel. "But I am striving to learn more of your holy book. I know that sura 60:7, for example, says, 'Allah will put friendship between you and those who have been your enemies. Allah is mighty, forgiving and merciful.' And sura 42:40 tells us, 'Whoever forgives and amends, he shall have his reward from Allah.'"

Dr. al-Montasser turned red and a vein stood out on his neck; I was sure he would either have a stroke or strangle me with his bare hands, whichever came first. "So," he screamed into my face, "you come to 'forgive' us? Is that your position? You have the audacity to come here and on our own soil—"

"No," I interjected, "not to offer our forgiveness—to ask you for *yours*."

THE PLACE FELL as silent as a tomb. Al-Montasser stared at me. He opened his mouth, then slowly closed it again without making a sound. I was sure that if I said another word, he would explode—but I had to go on.

"What I'm saying is, in the spirit of these and other suras of the Qur'an, and in the spirit of the teachings of Isa, I am asking your forgiveness for our country's killing of Colonel Qaddafi's daughter Hanna. The bombing raid that took her life happened during my service in Congress, and I feel complicit in this terrible event. I am so sorry."

He stared at me, mute and gaping. Had he not heard me?

"I want to offer my sincere apologies," I repeated. "And I hope you will convey them to the colonel as well."

The color drained from his face. He slumped back into his chair, still staring at me in disbelief. Without turning his head, he quietly barked a command to one of the aides stationed behind him. The man left the room and returned with a tray bearing a pot of tea and four cups.

We had been parched upon arrival, yet up until this moment we had not been offered so much as a sip of water—an absolutely extraordinary breach of diplomatic etiquette, and one clearly intended to send a message. I was never so grateful to see a cup of tea, and for more reasons than my thirst alone.

When Dr. al-Montasser began speaking again, his tone and demeanor had completely shifted. The manner in which our encounter unfolded from that point on was astonishing to witness. We spoke further about the Qur'an and about Islam, about the teachings of Jesus and the centuries of grave misunderstanding and mistrust between the different cultures of the world. We did not speak of politics or international dealings, not even for a single syllable.

At the end of an hour or so, we knew our audience was drawing to a close. Doug, who had contributed so many inspired comments during the meeting, offered to pray, and unbelievably, Dr. al-Montasser accepted, as if we had been colleagues and prayer partners for years. We stood with clasped hands and prayed.

At the end of our audience, as Dr. al-Montasser walked us to the door, he leaned toward me and quietly said, "You will have good news in ten days."

I glanced at him in surprise. "Whatever you do is completely up to you," I replied. "Just know that we are here to establish a small island of friendship in a sea of mistrust."

He nodded, and that was the end of our encounter.

Ten days later, Abdelbaset Ali Mohmed al-Megrahi and Al Amin Khalifa Fhimah, the Lockerbie suspects, were handed over for transport to the Netherlands to stand trial. Court proceedings began in May of the following year and concluded in February 2001 with the conviction of al-Megrahi, who is still serving a life sentence, and the acquittal of Fhimah.

A few months after our trip, a friend with connections to the intelligence community confided to me that we had been under surveillance the entire time we were traveling to Tripoli. We should have suspected as much.

"At first," my friend told me, "we thought you were crazy—in fact, we almost stopped you. We were afraid you were going to screw up all the work we'd put in on the Lockerbie Two for all these years. We thought, 'What the hell are these crazy bastards doing, thinking they can sneak in there in the middle of the night like James Bond and not make a mess of everything?'"

He paused just long enough to give me a chance to defend myself, in case I wanted to. I didn't even try. What could I say? He was right: we really had no idea what we were doing. All we had done was trust in the message we had to bring and in the impulse to offer friendship, with no strings attached. And at the height of a difficult encounter, I had apologized and asked for forgiveness. But I didn't say any of that. Instead, I just waited to see what else he had to say.

"But," he went on, "when they released Fhimah and Megrahi for extradition, our attitude changed. We stopped saying, 'What the hell did these guys think they were doing?'"

"Yeah?" I replied. "What did you say instead?"

He paused for a moment before replying and shook his head. "What the hell did these guys *do*?"

After our midnight flight to Tripoli, strange things happened in Libya. Later that year, Qaddafi pledged Libya's commitment to help fight al-Qaeda, and offered to voluntarily open his weapons program to international inspections. In fact, Qaddafi changed course rather dramatically, earning a reputation as a moderating figure, African elder statesman, and—of all things—humanitarian who has done much to improve the lives of poverty-stricken sub-Saharan Africans. He has been praised by—of all people—his longtime friend Nelson Mandela. Following the events of September 11, 2001, the fearsome Colonel Qaddafi made one of the first and strongest public condemnations of the attacks by any Muslim leader.

On May 15, 2006, the U.S. State Department announced that it would restore full diplomatic relations with Libya.

IN DECEMBER 1999, some eight months after our visit to Libya, the two men whose actions had so inspired me during that meeting joined together to do something extraordinary. Tony Hall and about a hundred other Americans traveled to Cotonou, Benin, to attend an international event, the Conference on Reconciliation and Development. In preparation for this historic event, Mathieu Kérékou invited the descendants of all African and European slave-trading nations to join him in making a public apology for the role of their ancestors in establishing and promulgating the Atlantic slave trade, and to seek the forgiveness of the African diaspora. Political leaders from several European nations and nearly fifty African nations attended the event.

Speaking before the group of some three hundred, Tony gave a brief talk in which he noted that more than three million Africans were sold into slavery from the shores of Benin alone. He apologized for the complicity of his own ancestors—and by extension, of his entire nation.

The following June, as part of introducing another version of his resolution (H. Con. Res. 356, "The Apology for Slavery Resolution of 2000"), he gave a compelling argument for the crucial importance of reconciliation and reported on his experience in Benin:

There are numerous reasons why Congress should apologize for its role in promoting and sustaining slavery. First, it is the right thing to do. If you offend your spouse or a friend, you have to say you are sorry in order to go forward in your relationship. It is so basic that we teach our kids from an early age—say you are sorry, or you can't play anymore; apologize, or you have to go to your room.

These three words—I am sorry—are a foundation for beginning again, a small price to pay for restoring lost trust, and a necessary first step in moving forward constructively.

This apology will not solve all of the problems, but it will begin new progress on issues that still divide Americans. It is never too late to admit a wrong and to ask for forgiveness. In giving those our nation wronged the dignity of this honest admission, we might all enjoy some measure of healing. And it will set the right example for our children. . . .

Last December, at the invitation of Benin's president, I attended a conference he convened on slavery and reconciliation. As I told the many dignitaries who attended, the tragedy of slavery and the curse that came with it will not simply disappear with time.

All of us live with the legacy of slavery. Africans' descendants suffer from the guilt of having sold their brothers and sisters, and the effects of exploitation. Europeans' descendants are cursed with a divided society, blind to the fact that our own privilege perpetuates that division, and unaware of the need to repent. And African-Americans are plagued by the remnants of the institution of slavery and the consequences of bitterness.

Apologizing is humbling. To admit to a wrong, you expose your wounds and warts for all the world to see. But the United States is a great country, and it should be big enough to admit its mistakes. And it should be wise enough to do whatever is necessary to heal its divisions. I believe this apology is faithful to our past, and essential to our future.[3]

It was one of the most extraordinary acts of reconciliation I'd ever seen.

Full Circle

Though our clandestine night flight to Libya was one of the strangest, most dramatic, and most humbling experiences of those years, it was not the height of my struggle with Jesus's actual teachings and the extent to which I was willing and able to put them into practice. That experience came during a visit, right here on American soil, with yet another leader in America's pantheon of global enemies. In fact, it happened mere miles from my home, in a Washington, D.C., suburb. And though I was in no physical danger this time, the struggle was far more difficult and cut far deeper. It was my first face-to-face encounter with my old nemesis, Yasser Arafat—an encounter that so strongly evoked feelings I'd held for years that I almost refused to let it take place.

Much as Qaddafi's position in the West has shifted dramatically over the years, so has Arafat's, only more so. The Reagan-era label of "international terrorist" softened considerably during the years that Bush senior was in the White House; by the time Clinton was in office, the PLO chairman had completed his transformation from militant to statesman and, incredibly, peacemaker.

In an address in December 1988, Arafat renounced terrorism "in all its forms, including state terrorism," and pledged recognition of Israel's right to exist. A few months later he was elected the first president of the newly formed independent state of Palestine. From that office he engaged in secret negotiations with Israel, leading to the Oslo Accords of September 1993. That same month, in his capacity as chairman of the Palestine Liberation Organization (PLO), Arafat signed documents that officially renounced violence and recognized the state of Israel. In response, Israel's prime minister Yitzhak Rabin officially recognized the PLO. In December 1994 Arafat, together with Rabin and Israeli foreign minister Shimon Peres, was awarded the Nobel Peace Prize. In his acceptance speech, Arafat quoted the Qur'an: "If the enemy incline towards peace, do thou incline towards peace, and trust in Allah" (sura 8:61).

IN JANUARY 1999 I was approached by a close Lebanese friend named Nassim Matar. Nassim had been involved in the Israeli-Palestinian conflict for years, and had been one of the players behind the scenes who had helped bring the two parties together. He and his wife, Maha, a Palestinian, had even attended an event on the White House lawn in 1993 with Yitzhak Rabin and Yasser Arafat, marking their historic signing of the Declaration of Principles for Peace.

"Mark," Nassim told me excitedly, "Arafat is coming to America next month! We want to throw a private dinner in his honor. Would you be willing to host the dinner?"

I felt my breath catch. Me, host a dinner for Arafat? Out of the question!

The world had changed a lot over the fifteen years since that team of CIA and FBI agents showed up in my congressional office with a bulletproof vest hidden in a briefcase. During that time, I had been through a good deal of change myself. But I still had a gut-level hostility and distrust regarding this man. Hearing that someone has put out a contract on one's life makes an impression that doesn't readily fade.

Nassim, of course, had no idea of the history between me and the chairman. I quickly recovered my composure and told him I would consider it. But I was only stalling for time, until I could find some way to get out of this. There was no way I was going to participate in an event to honor this man, let alone serve as host to such a thing.

That night I had a terrible dream. It was as if God were showing me a PowerPoint presentation tracing the story of all those who were the targets of arms I had helped secure for Cold War allies during my tenure in Congress. No doubt, many of those arms were used to kill the innocent. How often had I bragged about my support for what we back then termed freedom fighters? The faces of the women and children I dreamt about that night, who may well have been killed by the weapons I promoted, were burned into my mind's eye.

I awoke with an awful thought: *Siljander, you're a hypocrite!* I had condemned Arafat for having blood on his hands. But what about the blood on my own? Was forgiveness truly possible—for him, for myself? For any of us? I didn't see how, in good faith, I could refuse this occasion to build a bridge of friendship with this old enemy of mine. If this wasn't the ultimate opportunity to live the values of Jesus's teachings, then what was?

The next morning I called Nassim and agreed to host the dinner. After I hung up the phone, I sat back in my chair and pondered the enormity of what I had just agreed to—and the even more awful fact that I was so conflicted about the whole thing.

Wasn't I the one who had met with President al-Bashir, not only once but several times? Hadn't I sat with Muammar Qaddafi's foreign minister and asked *him* for forgiveness?

Yes, but the whole "love thine enemies" idea was all very well when it was still played out to some extent in an abstract context. I had no family killed in Sudan's civil war, no personal friends who had died at Qaddafi's hands. As much as I hated to admit it, none of my many encounters with Muslim statesmen over the years had challenged me to my core the way the prospect of hosting this dinner was tearing at me now. Al-Bashir, Qaddafi, and the others had been America's enemies. Arafat was my *personal* enemy. The man had tried to have me killed!

But I'd committed to it; clearly I couldn't back out, even if I wanted to. If I backed out, how would I face my friends? How would I face myself?

WE HELD THE dinner at a private home in a D.C. suburb. It was the wildest thing that neighborhood had ever seen. About sixty people were in attendance, but the presence of security forces from the Secret Service, Mossad, and Palestinian Secret Police more than doubled that number. Men were stationed around the house at ten-foot intervals, all armed with Uzis or submachine guns. At the end of the street, a car was turned on its side to form a barrier, as if we were in the middle of a war zone. Two helicopters flew overhead, circling the house, and Navy Seals offered protection from the nearby Potomac River. This was supposed to be a quiet suburban community. The neighbors were not happy.

Yet there was good reason for the epic levels of security. For one thing, Arafat was accompanied in his visit by none other than Leah Rabin, widow of Arafat's fellow Nobel laureate, Yitzhak Rabin.

In the wake of the Oslo Accords, both Rabin and Arafat were regarded as traitors by many of their own people. In November 1995, barely a year after receiving the Nobel Peace Prize, Rabin was shot dead at a peace rally by a young Israeli who later said that Rabin had been intent on "giving our country to the Arabs" and that he hoped by his actions to derail the peace process. Rabin's widow had bravely continued in her husband's mission, not only affirming her support of the accords but even going so far as to travel with Arafat and participate in public appearances with him.

And Leah Rabin was far from the only security risk. Arafat himself was no stranger to the assassin's plot. Indeed, Western observers were often amazed at his ability to survive, and marveled that over the years of violence and shifting loyalties in the Mideast and Africa, he had time and again managed to avoid the numerous attempts on his life. It was not at all unreasonable to view the presence of Arafat and Mrs. Rabin together in one setting, on American soil, as an event warranting unusual security precautions.

For me, the potential threat to life and limb was not the most consuming concern of the evening. I knew that sooner or later I was going to confront the chairman himself. What would that meeting be like? I didn't see how I could look the man in the face without betraying my long-standing feelings of antipathy and hostility.

Sure enough, in the course of the evening, the inevitable occurred. As host of the event, I found myself sitting side by side with Yasser Arafat. To my astonishment, the figure we had so roundly condemned throughout the 1980s turned out to be quite a gracious and charming man. We fell into easy conversation.

After fifteen or twenty minutes, Chairman Arafat's speechwriter and confidant, Saeb Erakat (who also held the rank of prime minister), took me aside and mentioned that Arafat was scheduled to speak the next day at a large luncheon to an audience composed mostly of Christians who were there as part of the National Prayer Breakfast. He had heard through Nassim that I "knew something about Jesus in the Qur'an" and wondered if he could beg my assistance.

Well of course, I ventured. In what way could I possibly assist him?

In Chairman Arafat's address, he said, he wanted to discuss the common bond that Muslims and Christians share in the person of Jesus—or Isa, as he was called in the Qur'an. (I nodded. Yes, I was familiar with the Arabic nomenclature.) He wondered, could I perhaps help him find a few appropriate suras to use in his talk?

I glanced over at Arafat, who was talking with the guests and glancing over at me every now and then. Here he was, my Muslim enemy. And his aide was asking me for my help—with the Qur'an. I looked back at Saeb. "Of course," I replied, trying not to betray how dazed I felt. "What have you got so far?"

He showed me a selection of a few suras he had gotten from Nassim. We reviewed them. I made some suggestions. We settled on six suras for the chairman to choose from.

The next day I attended the luncheon. When Arafat got up to speak, I was on the edge of my seat, wondering which of the suras he might use or whether he would remember to use any of them. He did—in fact, he quoted *all six* of them, and when he came to those points in the text that referred directly to Isa, he substituted the phrase "Our Lord Jesus Christ," causing quite a few murmurs of astonishment in his audience. This surprised me, too: Muslims almost never use "Lord" as a title for anyone other than Allah.

As I sat listening to the president of the Palestinian Authority speak, the full significance of the moment slammed into me and nearly took my breath away. Here I was, sitting at the International Luncheon session of the National Prayer Breakfast, exactly fifteen years since I had stormed out of this same event when a Muslim statesman had dared to stand before our group and read from the Qur'an. That had been just a few months after learning that Arafat had put out a contract on my life.

And now I sat in the same Washington hotel, listening in rapt attention as another Muslim statesman—the very man who had allegedly arranged for my assassination—stood before our group and read from the Qur'an . . . in fact, read text that *I had helped pick out for him.*

• • •

THE ENCOUNTER WITH Arafat brought home to me the central lesson I was learning: if we're going to find any viable common ground between our faiths, cultures, and nations, if we are going to build workable bridges across the Muslim-Christian divide, *it has to be personal*. It's possible to arbitrate a cease-fire agreement or oversee the drafting of a provisional coalition charter with a good degree of arms-length emotional detachment—but we can't build a friendship that way. Negotiating with an enemy may be a professional act; *loving* one's enemy is personal.

I'd also come to see that it's one thing to establish an initial connection with someone in a foreign land; it's quite another to maintain that connection and create a genuine friendship that builds, grows, and deepens over time. In Congress I'd seen how conventional diplomacy works: we tend to come in with a flourish, make our demands, then head back to our hotels, pack our bags, and be on the next plane to D.C. This had to be different. Here, the point was not to present an agenda but to build relationships. You can't communicate once and then assume the message will stick. A relationship is like a child. You don't give birth to a child and then leave him in his crib and say, "Here's our number, call us if you need us, it's been great having you." You stay in touch! When you create a relationship, it's a long-term commitment. It takes *continuity*.

A few years earlier, after our first Sudan visit, I had contacted Dr. al-Shingieti, the Sudanese diplomat who originally set up the meeting, and invited him and his American wife, Iman (which in Arabic means Faith), to come to our home in Virginia. They joined us for dinner, and the four of us hit it off like old friends. They also brought their kids along, who had a blast playing with our kids. We soon had a second visit, and then a third, going back and forth to each other's homes. We became fast friends and have remained so to this day.

My friendship with Abubaker al-Shingieti soon took on the character of a research partnership. Whenever we got together, our conversation invariably turned to matters of the Qur'an and the Bible, so we began to set aside small blocks of time here and there to study together. I fondly recall the two of us sitting together, kneeling on his living room floor with books spread out all around us, hunting through the texts like a pair of Indiana Joneses poring through never-before-seen artifacts in a long-forgotten jungle. I'd say, "Hey, couldn't this sura mean something different than how your culture has been interpreting it? I mean, couldn't this word actually mean this, instead of that?" And he'd say, "Well, I suppose it could, there's no reason why not—perhaps we just never considered it before." The two of us became joint explorers, mutual teachers and students in a study of the common ground between our faiths—a common ground that seemed to grow larger the more we explored it.

After returning from Libya, we were likewise determined not to let the meeting remain an isolated event. It was critical that we follow up and invest in the kind of continuity that genuine relationships demand. We made contact with Dr. Ali Abdussalam Treky, a longtime senior diplomat who was Qaddafi's former foreign minister and then permanent representative to the United Nations (today he serves as Libya's chief of African affairs). Dr. Treky couldn't travel to see us, because U.S. sanctions put a twenty-five-mile travel ban on all ambassadors or diplomats from sanctioned countries, which meant he couldn't leave New York City. But that didn't stop us from going to see him. During that nail-biting Tripoli visit, we had assured the foreign minister that time would prove our overtures to friendship, and we were determined not to let too much time pass before we followed up.

Along with David Laux, a close friend and former member of the National Security Council, I met with Dr. Treky over several meals. We told him about our mission—to establish relationships of collegial friendship, with no agenda and no political strings attached—and he was fascinated. We shared with him in some detail some of our textual and linguistic findings concerning the Qur'an and Injil, Arabic and Aramaic, and he was intrigued. "This is revolutionary stuff," he said. "Why don't we know about this?"

And thus began a long-term friendship that, like that with Abubaker al-Shingieti, has continued to this day.

THOSE FEW MOMENTS spent with Yasser Arafat's speechwriter, poring over a few texts from the Qur'an and discussing their meaning, significance, and possible impact in a speech to an international audience the following day, stayed with me for days, for months. Every time I had the opportunity to sit with a new Muslim friend, comb through the holy books, and talk about our beliefs, I felt it stretch me—and more and more, I could think of nothing I could possibly be doing that would be more valuable than giving myself over to that stretching.

Meanwhile, the chasm of misunderstanding between Eastern and Western societies widened and deepened with each passing year. Tension between the two worlds continued to intensify, erupting in a steady rhythm of violent outbursts that seemed to drum a crescendo toward an inevitable clash of awful proportions.

June 25, 1996: A fuel truck idling by Building #131 of the Khobar Towers housing complex in Saudi Arabia explodes, killing nineteen American servicemen and one Saudi and injuring 372 others. The bomb is alleged to have been planted and detonated by members of Hezbollah, the Iran-backed Lebanese militia group.

August 7, 1998: Two simultaneous car bombs explode at the U.S. embassies in the East African capital cities of Dar es

Salaam, Tanzania, and Nairobi, Kenya, killing 225 and injuring over four thousand. The carefully coordinated attack is linked to al-Qaeda, bringing the group and its leader, Osama bin Laden, to public attention for the first time and placing bin Laden on the FBI's Ten Most Wanted list.

October 12, 2000: The USS *Cole*, a guided missile destroyer docked for refueling in a Yemen harbor, is struck by a small boat carrying two men and several hundred pounds of explosives. The blast blows a forty-foot hole in the boat's side and kills seventeen U.S. sailors.

Each of these events, along with the various other smaller and less publicized terrorist attacks of those years, was a tragedy in its own right. Yet to me they added up to something larger and more terrible still. It felt as if there were an invisible, barely audible clock ticking behind the surface of events. Or perhaps the sound was the quiet sizzling of a fuse burning down to impact.

Malcolm Kalp's words continued echoing in my ears—*We have no idea what we're up against*—and his prediction seemed more telling with every passing month.

My layman's grasp of the Qur'an and discoveries of common ground and bridges that we'd catalogued had served us well in establishing rapport and rapprochement with heads of state and key diplomatic players on the world stage. These experiences had also stretched my own identity as a man of faith and follower of Jesus. But more and more, I felt the inadequacy of my understanding. Or perhaps it was that the depths of hostility, misunderstanding, and alienation around me were simply looming ever larger, and the call for a greater level of insight was becoming more insistent.

In between the trips around the world, my friends and I threw ourselves into intensive study of the holy books with a deepening sense of urgency. We began interacting with dozens of

Muslim and Christian scholars, linguists, pastors, imams,[1] and others, poring through texts and discussing our findings. Often I found myself sitting alone on my living room floor, surrounded by piles of reference books, deep into the early morning hours. There were more answers here, I felt sure of it, and they desperately needed to be found.

Pillars and Bridges

Stepping out of the dust and debris of my paradigm crash of 1987, I had spent more than a decade exploring this strange new territory where the Bible and Qur'an seemed to point to similar truths and common human values. However, I had not yet arrived at a clear sense of exactly how the different faiths fit together, of what all these discoveries really meant. I had let go of the parameters of my old worldview but had not yet quite found the clear coordinates of a new one.

One evening in mid-1999, I made the first in a series of startling discoveries that moved my journey a giant step forward.

It started, as so many of these discoveries do, with a point that troubled me, a common issue of conflict that Christians and Jews have with Islam: according to the Qur'an, Abraham, Moses, and Jesus *were all Muslims*. Abraham, in fact, is often referred to in Islamic cultures as "the first Muslim." Not surprisingly, Christians and Jews are highly offended by this assertion. But there's no getting around it: the Qur'an does say it, and Muslims recite it. I wanted to know, what does the Qur'an really mean by that? What does "being a Muslim" actually mean?

Thus I found myself at my desk, late at night, surrounded by books on Islam, along with my well-worn copies of the Bible, Peshitta (Aramaic New Testament), and Qur'an, parsing through explanations of the Five Pillars of Islam, the core practices that define the life of the faithful Muslim.

Shahada (Testimony of Faith)

"There is no God but Allah, and Muhammad is the messenger of Allah." In Arabic: *lā ilāha i llā Llāh; muhammadun rasūl Allāh.*

This is the Shahada, the central declaration of faith of the Islamic creed. Sincere recitation of the Shahada (ideally in the presence of at least two witnesses, though this is not mandatory) is considered the condition of entering the Islamic faith. This declaration is meant to express one's belief that there is no higher purpose to life than serving and obeying Allah, and that this is achieved through following the teachings of the last of God's prophets, Muhammad.

Salat (Prayer)

Salat refers to the obligatory daily prayers of Islam, which are traditionally practiced five times a day. This is much like the "canonical hours" or "offices" of the early Christian church, which were increments of time between prescribed prayer, typically eight daily prayer events plus three or four nightly divisions ("vigils"). Still practiced by some Christian orders today, these practices were derived from the Jewish practice of reciting prayers at set times of day. ("Seven times a day do I praise thee because of thy righteous judgments," says the longest psalm in the Bible [Psalms 119:164].)

In the Muslim version, prayers are said at dawn, midday, late afternoon, sunset, and nightfall. The five prescribed prayers consist of suras from the Qur'an and are said in Arabic; as in Judaism, they are accompanied by movement of the body. In Islamic tradition, there is no one to pray for you or act as an intermediary between the individual and God. The individual Muslim says his prayers daily, whether alone or in a mosque, in direct communication with Allah.

Zakat (Charitable Giving)

Muslims believe, much as Christians do, that everything belongs to God, and that wealth is therefore not owned by human beings but rather held in trust. Our own possessions are purified and blessed by the practice of setting aside a portion for our society, and especially for those in need. The word *zakat* means both "purification" and "growth."

Much like the Jewish and Christian tithe, the Muslim *zakat* is calculated in private and with autonomy; although there are guidelines, they are given with an understanding of flexibility in the individual application. In fact, as was true in traditional Judaic culture, considerable leeway is given in the interpretation of charitable giving.

Sawm (Fasting)

Every year, during the month of Ramadan, all Muslims fast from dawn until sundown, abstaining from food, drink, and sexual relations. As with *zakat*, there is considerable leeway to accommodate individual circumstance, for the elderly or the infirm, or for travel.

Hajj (Pilgrimage)

Every year, over two million people travel to the Ka'aba, the small cubical building now surrounded by the Sacred Mosque in Mecca, Saudi Arabia, as fulfillment of their requirement of hajj. However, the idea of hajj, like that of *zakat* and *sawm*, is more liberal than many realize. The annual pilgrimage is an obligation only for those physically and financially able to do so.

The principle of hajj is that the faithful are encouraged to make pilgrimages to holy sites, much the way Jews traditionally returned to Jerusalem for Pesach (Passover) and Christians today travel to Jerusalem, the Vatican, and other holy sites when possible.

As I sorted through explanations of the Five Pillars of Islam, it struck me that at their core, none of these practices seemed really incompatible with being a good Christian or a good Jew. Some Westerners are put off by the term "Allah," but as I'd learned six years earlier when I first began reading the Qur'an, this is simply the Arabic word for God. Some twenty million Christian Arabs pray to *Allah* every day, and Jesus himself, along with all his followers, used the nearly identical Aramaic version of the word, *Alaha*, when he spoke about God.

There are other potential roadblocks, of course. Ramadan, Mecca, the Ka'aba: these are foreign terms and concepts to the Christian or Jewish faithful in the West. But they are unessential details, cultural specifics not to be confused with the essence of the pillars themselves. Fasting for purity of mind and soul is fasting for purity of mind and soul, regardless of the name one applies to the time of fasting.

What's more, the five pillars are not of equal status: the first, Shahada, is central and takes precedence over all the other four. When I would ask my Muslim friends, "What constitutes being a Muslim? If one wanted to become a Muslim, what would one actually have to do?" they would tell me, "You say the Shahada. You practice the five pillars, day in and day out, but in essence, the core of it is that you say the Shahada—not only with your mouth forming the words, but that you say it in your heart and mean it with your whole being. If you do that, then you are a Muslim."

As I sat pondering this, a thought occurred to me: this being the case, then no wonder the Qur'an speaks of Abraham as being "the first Muslim"! Abraham's unswerving faith in and submission to the one God was the single most distinguishing feature of his career. To Jews and Christians alike, it stood as one of the central models of behavior and inspiration. The apostle Paul waxed enthusiastic about the faith of Abraham, frequently quoting from Genesis: "Abraham believed in God, and it was counted to him for righteousness."[1]

Indeed, Abraham's radical monotheistic faith was the central story point of Genesis, and is arguably the fulcrum upon which all three faiths—Judaism, Christianity, and Islam—rest. And it was easy to see that, like Abraham, both Moses and Jesus were submitted and surrendered to the one God.

But what about this business of Muhammad being the messenger of Allah? Once again, this didn't seem to present a fundamental conflict of principle. Nothing in either Judaism or Christianity contraindicates acknowledging Muhammad as a prophet or "messenger of God." From Job to Elijah to Malachi to John the Baptist to Paul the apostle, both traditions are rich in such "messengers." Many Christian sects, particularly Pentecostals, believe there are living prophets today who at times speak the "word of God" or truths that can be verified in the Bible.

While many Muslims and Christians believe to some extent in the infallibility of all the prophets, they were still human beings, often exhibiting questionable behavior (from adultery to murder and acts of war), and were just as flawed and sinful as the rest of us. Yet this didn't detract from their being used as messengers for God's words. The Qur'an actually points out that among prophets, Jesus was uniquely "righteous," "pure," or sinless (sura 19:19)—yet I cannot find where this is said of any other prophet, not even Muhammad.

Whether one believes that the Qur'an was dictated to Muhammad by the archangel Gabriel, when one considers that his recitation testified to hundreds of concepts that echo the Torah—including reference to angels, heaven, hell, Adam and

Eve, Abraham, Moses, and others—one would be hard-pressed not to acknowledge his words as being in the tradition of the prophetic verses concerning the doings of God. What Muhammad had to say about Jesus is absolutely overwhelming. Regardless of what one might think of Muhammad's specific standing in the great scheme of things, it seems pretty clear that what he set down forms a very close parallel to the tradition of Jeremiah, Isaiah, John, and James.

Of course neither Abraham, nor Moses, nor Jesus ever mentioned Muhammad; they all predated his birth by hundreds or thousands of years. Yet this does not disqualify them from being declared "Muslims" by no less an authority than the Qur'an itself.

If we then set aside for a moment the provision about Muhammad being God's messenger and focus on the message embodied in the five pillars themselves, here's what we have:

"I believe in one God."
"I will pray every day."
"I will give to the poor and needy, according to my ability."
"I will fast and do my best to purify my body and soul."
"I will travel, in body if possible and in mind and spirit otherwise, to holy sites to celebrate my God."

What Christian or Jew could object to any of these five statements? Was it too much, then, to say that a good Christian or Jew, adhering to his own faith in all ways and also following all five of these central tenets, could at the same time be considered a Muslim, at least in principle? As bizarre as it sounded—and to a lifelong follower of Jesus like myself, it sounded pretty bizarre—I could not see any flaw in the logic.

I sat at my desk, turning this thought over, looking for flaws and finding none. And then it occurred to me to come at it from the other direction. What if we examined the core tenets of being a practicing Christian or practicing Jew—how incompatible were *they* with being a practicing Muslim? Which begged the question: what *are* the central tenets of being a practicing Christian or Jew?

WHEN THE RELIGIOUS leaders of the day were testing Jesus and trying to trick him into contradicting scripture and so exposing himself as a heretic, they posed this question: "Which is the greatest commandment?" And everyone knows what he answered. . . .

Except that, curiously enough, when you ask Christians what he answered, nine times out of ten they miss the *beginning* of his answer. The answer you typically get is the one from Matthew, which is not incorrect—it's just incomplete. Most Christians will tell you that he said, "Love the Lord your God with all your heart and with all your soul and with all your might and with all your mind" (Matt. 22:37).

But Mark's Gospel includes a critical detail in the exchange. Let's not forget that Jesus was a rabbi, and indeed, by all accounts was an exceptionally dedicated and accomplished rabbi who knew the Torah inside and out. He repeatedly insisted that he meant to uphold and fulfill the Jewish scriptures, not to contradict or supersede them.

> Do not suppose that I have come to weaken the law [Torah] or the prophets; I have not come to weaken, but to fulfill. (Matt. 5:17)

In other words, Jesus saw his own teaching not as a departure from Judaic tradition but as an unbroken continuation of that tradition—just as Muhammad evidently saw the Qur'an and his own teaching as a continuation of the existing scriptures.

We gave Moses the Book and followed him up with a succession of Messengers. [sura 2:87] . . . We make no distinction between one and another of His messengers. [sura 2:285] . . . Before this We wrote the Zubor [Psalms], after the Turat [Torah]. [sura 21:105]

When Jesus was challenged by the Pharisees to name the greatest commandment, according to Mark, he replied:

The first [i.e., greatest] of all commandments is this: *Hear, O Israel:* the Lord our God is one Lord; and you must love the Lord your God with all your heart and with all your soul and with all your mind and with all your might; this is the first commandment. (Mark 12:29–30, emphasis added)

These initial words, *Hear, O Israel*—the words Mark includes— are critical. They make it unequivocally clear that Jesus was quoting directly from Deuteronomy 6:3–4, the famous passage called the Shema, which is still recited every day, morning and evening, by practicing Jews around the world. The word *Shema,* which is usually translated as "hear," also means "to proclaim, to witness, or to testify"—

Wait a moment! I turned back to my other texts on the Shahada. What was the derivation of that word? I flitted hurriedly through several pages and found what I was looking for: the word *Shahada* means "to proclaim, to witness, or to testify."

Exactly the same as the definition of *Shema.*

Shema. Shahada.

"The Lord our God [Aramaic: *Alaha*] is one." "There is no god but Allah."

The central declaration of faith—as Jesus put it, "The first of all the commandments." They were the same thing. They used very nearly the same *word.*

By this time I was pacing the living room, my hands trembling with excitement and astonishment. The central profession of faith of all three great monotheistic, Abrahamic faiths, faiths whose followers have battled and warred and fought for centuries upon centuries, were not simply compatible—they were essentially *identical*.

Could this possibly be? Jews and Muslims? I thought about my experiences on the Green Line of Lebanon, of being nearly shot to death by a Muslim Palestinian and Jewish Israeli on the same afternoon. What would those two soldiers think if they knew that their entire ways of life rested upon the profession of central beliefs that not only were *not* at war but were in essence *one and the same?*

The Judeo-Christian West and Muslim East. Isaac and Ishmael. *Shema. Shahada.*

I SAT BACK down at my desk to think through the implications of what I'd stumbled upon. Jesus didn't stop with the Shema. The Pharisees had asked him only for one commandment, but he went on to explain *what he understood this to mean* by way of giving them a second, this time quoting from Leviticus:

> And the second is like to it, You must love your neighbor as yourself. There is no other commandment greater than these. (Mark 12:31, quoting Lev. 19:18)

This was the radical understanding that he amplified throughout his ministry, but especially in the Sermon on the Mount and in the Gospel of John (as reflected also in the later letters of John), as the famous "love commandment."

> A new commandment I give you, that you love one another; just as I have loved you, that you also love one another. By

this every man shall know that you are my disciples, if you have love one for another. (John 13:34–35)

According to John, in that intimate setting only hours before his capture by Roman soldiers, Jesus described this as "a new commandment," as if to give it a special emphasis and clear distinction that his followers would not possibly forget. But of course, in Jesus's mind it was clearly not a "new" commandment at all: he had already quoted it from Leviticus. What was new was what Jesus said this simple injunction really meant. Notice the phrase "like to it" in the above passage from Mark:

And the second is *like to it*: "You must love your neighbor as yourself."

In other words, Jesus explains that he is citing a second commandment ("Love your neighbor as yourself") because it *is related to* the first ("Love God with all your heart, soul, mind and power").

I was back up on my feet now, pacing again. I could feel some insight here, working its way to the surface.

To Jesus, loving God and submitting to his will were exemplified by the act of submitting ourselves to the godliness in one another. To love one's neighbor—including one's enemy—as oneself was not simply good civics or pragmatic social etiquette, it was the very evidence of having an attitude of submission to God. He makes this abundantly clear in the Sermon on the Mount:

I say to you, Love your enemies, bless anyone who curses you, do good to anyone who hates you, and pray for those who carry you away by force and persecute you, *so that you may become sons of your Father who is in heaven*, who causes his sun to shine upon the good and the bad, and who pours down his rain upon the just and upon the unjust. . . . *There-fore become perfect, just as your Father in heaven is perfect.* (Matt. 5:44–48, emphasis added)

In other words, we are enjoined to treat our enemies with un-conditional goodwill, not simply because it's a noble thing to do but *because that's what God does.* Doing so is the essence of sub-mitting to God's will, because unconditional love is God's agenda. When we love our neighbor (including our enemy), we are, to use modern parlance, getting on the same page with God. We are getting with the program.

Jesus was defining what he meant when he urged his follow-ers to go "convert" the world, to cause people to *shalem* (surren-der). Teach people to love God, he was saying, to *shalem* (surrender) with everything you have—your heart, your pas-sion, your mind, intellect, emotion, body, strength, and actions toward others—to your neighbors. That, said Jesus, was total surrender, total *shalem*—

And that's when it hit me. That word. I stopped pacing and stood, transfixed.

Shalem. It was the word that had so shaken my world when I first discovered it back in 1991, thumbing through the Peshitta and beginning to learn Aramaic. Hebrew: *Shalom.* Arabic: *Salaam.* Aramaic: *Shalem.*

Shalem: submit to God. *Shalem*: be at peace. *Shalem*: be surren-dered. *Mu shalem* = one who is surrendered.

Mu-shalem.

Muslim.

By all accounts, Muhammad was not a literate man prior to his revelations. He grew up in a culture rich in oral tradition, and he knew his traditions well but by hearing them spoken, not by reading them on parchments. He was surrounded by devoted people, a few of them Christians, all of whom would have known and recited their Injil (New Testament) in Aramaic. Muhammad had been steeped in this text. When Jesus spoke about being surrendered to God, Muhammad heard his words in the language in which he had originally spoken them: *Shalem*.

Islam and Christianity were not simply *overlapping* ideas. They were not merely *compatible*. In the most central sense, *they were one continuum*. Muhammad had named his movement of total submission to God by identifying it with the core message of Jesus and his followers—even to the point of using the very same Aramaic word: *shalem*.

Sura 3:19 of the Qur'an says, "The religion before Allah is Islam (submission to His will)." The Arabic word translated as "religion" is *deen*, which a most respected Sudanese *sheikh*[2] told me refers not to membership in an exclusive "club" but to a *state of being*: in this case, a state of being in submission (Islam) to God (Allah).

Christianity was not intended by its founder as a new religion, with strict rules, regulations, structures, and hierarchies, but as a continuity with and recovery of the essence of the old one. And the exact same thing is true of Islam.

Neither was meant to be a political body of beliefs and doctrines one would join by converting *to*. They were both meant as an intensely personal return to one's true self, to one's complete submission to the Creator. They were intended as movements, peaceful revolutions of the human heart. And they had an identical mission and agenda, right down to the very words: *Repent and be converted. Submit to God. Be at peace. Be one—"mu"—who is surrendered—"shalem." Mu-shalem. Muslim.*

No wonder the Qur'an declared that Abraham, Moses, and Jesus were all Muslims. So, in the sense of the fundamental meaning of the word, were all practicing Christians and Jews. Were there differences between these three Abrahamic faiths? Of course, and I wasn't so naïve as to think that they could—or should—be merged, or their distinctions whittled away to nothing. Yet there appeared to be far more common ground here than most of us had ever thought possible.

Abraham, Moses, Jesus, James, Paul, Muhammad: though from disparate cultures and faiths, all were of fundamentally the *same substance* of faith. And so, as near as I could tell, was I.

ELEVEN

A Hug from His Holiness

Not long after stumbling upon these discoveries about the Shema and Shahada and the derivation of the word "Muslim," I had an altogether unexpected opportunity to see just how broadly the universality of the person of Jesus—the representation of the "Word of God"—can bring together not only Christians and Muslims but people of many other religions and faiths as well.

Earlier in 1999, a member of the Indian parliament came to Washington one day and joined us at our weekly ambassadors' breakfast. As the conversation went around the table, some of us talked about the different sorts of prayer groups we were engaged in, and he spoke up. "You know, we've tried to get a parliamentary prayer group together in India like the one you have here and those you've told us about in other countries, but it doesn't seem to work. There are too many conflicts within the group. How do you manage it here?"

I wasn't sure how to answer, so I used the diplomat's best rhetorical tool: answer a question with another question.

"What are you using as the basis of your coming together?" I asked him.

"We tried nationalism," he explained, "and that didn't work, because everyone has different views of that. We tried God, and that was even tougher. The Buddhists aren't really big on God. The Sikhs believe in one God, but the Hindus have so many gods you can't keep count, and the Muslims were upset because the Hindus might be thinking of a different God ... so that didn't work. We tried everything we could think of and couldn't figure out a way to make it work. How do you guys do it?"

I knew how we worked here in our own cultural context, but he was working within a very different context. The picture he was describing made the conflicts among the Abrahamic faiths seem simple by comparison! I wasn't entirely sure if our approach would apply directly to the other side of the world, so I again answered his question with a question:

"Have you ever tried coming together around the ideas of Jesus?"

No, he said, they had not tried that. In fact, it had never occurred to them.

This intrigued me. I pursued the question further. "Is there anyone in that group," I asked him, "Sikh, Hindu, Buddhist, Muslim, Christian, *anyone* who would be offended by focusing your talks around Jesus? I don't mean Christianity, but Jesus himself. In other words, if you removed all the religious trappings and simply talked about the historical person and what he taught?"

He thought about this. "I guess not," he finally said. "Buddhists love Jesus. Hindus certainly think he's one of the gods. Christians obviously think he's the son of God. And Muslims say he's a prophet."

Now I was fascinated. "Why don't you try it?" I suggested.

A little later that year I heard from my Indian friend. He told me that they had tried doing exactly what we had talked about, and to his delight it had worked beautifully. They now had a parliamentary group of nearly two dozen members from all the faiths we'd mentioned, meeting and praying together regularly and even holding conferences where they invited in outside guests.

This was exciting. But soon it got more so: in October of that year, a few months after I had had that epiphany about the Shema and Shahada, they invited me to attend one of these conferences as their guest. I would have the chance to witness this experiment in the universality of Jesus firsthand!

The group convened in the ancient city of Agra, home of the Taj Mahal. Consisting of members of parliament from the various nations of South Asia, it was a colorful mix that included members of the world's five most populous religions: Christians, Muslims, Buddhists, Hindus, and Sikhs, all meeting together and praying together with great success. There were parliament members and cabinet officials from Bangladesh, Nepal, Sri Lanka, and Bhutan, and the Dalai Lama had sent two cabinet members to participate as well.

For the next three days, I sat spellbound in the audience as they talked about Jesus. Not so much about Christianity as an organized institution or religion—just Jesus the person, and the astonishingly radical things he taught. They spoke about the Sermon on the Mount, the beatitudes—the blessed peacemakers, the meek who shall inherit the earth—and about the "love" commandment. They talked about how these teachings had filtered around the world down through the centuries, inspiring countless charitable movements, humanitarian efforts, and the dedication of millions to helping improve the lot of a struggling humanity.

This was no revival meeting or cheering session for any particular denomination or religion. A collection of political parliamentarians had funded the whole event themselves and even paid for our hotel rooms and meals, so that about a hundred people could sit for three days and talk about the teachings and person of Jesus. No one was offended. No one got upset. It was one of the most captivating, powerful events I've ever attended.

During a break on the first full day of the conference, a few of us who were sitting together decided to take a walk outside.

We were staying at the Jaypee Palace, a beautiful new hotel that featured a series of gorgeous, hand-sculpted gardens right off the conference room. A handful of us headed out into the gardens.

The weather was beautiful, and at first we were all lost in thought. As we walked, we began talking about all that we'd heard that morning. We made a circuit of the gardens and then, just as we found ourselves back at the entrance and about to return to the conference hall, one person said, "Say, before we go back in, why don't we pray?"

The five of us held hands and prayed. After we finished praying we were silent for a moment, and then suddenly one of our party, a gentleman with a soulful face beneath a pure white turban, exclaimed, "Hey! You notice something?"

"Notice what?" I replied.

"You, Siljander, you're a Christian." In fact, by this time I had reached the point where I no longer tended to identify myself by that designation, especially when outside my Western confines. But I let that go and didn't make an issue out of it. After all, I certainly came from a strong Christian background; and I was still passionately devoted to Jesus and very much a "follower of the Way," much as Paul, Peter, or James would have understood and related to the term. "Okay," I agreed.

"I'm a Sikh," he went on. "And look"—he gestured at our companions one by one. "He's a Buddhist" (this was a member of the Dalai Lama's cabinet), "and he's a Hindu" (this was a member of the Indian parliament), "and he" (pointing to a member of cabinet from Bangladesh)—"he's a Muslim!"

He was right. Although it was completely unintentional and had not been planned or orchestrated by any one of us, it just happened that we five had gotten together for a walk through the gardens, a chat about life, spirit, and the world, and a prayer together—and we did indeed represent five completely different faiths.

I felt a chill run through me. This was no theoretical construct or theological concept—this was living, breathing common ground that had shown up in our midst with complete spontaneity. Glancing at my comrades' faces, I could see that the moment was having a similar impact on all of us.

"Under what other auspices but the name Jesus," I wondered aloud, "could five such diverse people hold hands and pray together without experiencing even the slightest sense of conflict or incompatibility?" They all agreed that this was indeed extraordinary, and on that note, we reentered the hotel and went on with the conference.

But it didn't end there. The Buddhist reported back to the Dalai Lama and described this little vignette of the five of us praying together in the gardens of the Jaypee Palace Hotel. The Dalai Lama himself then invited a small group of the assembled parliamentarians to visit him—and when they received the invitation, they in turn invited me to come, not just as an observer but as part of the delegation. In fact, they invited me to *lead* the delegation.

"But you are all active, sitting members of parliaments and cabinets," I protested, "and I'm only a former congressman. I haven't held office for quite a few years!"

But they insisted. "You're from America," they said, "and you have a unique perspective. You should lead the group."

While reluctant to accept their invitation as leader, I was thrilled to be going with them and eventually agreed. When the conference concluded, we packed our bags and headed north toward the Tibetan border for our rendezvous with Tenzin Gyatso, the fourteenth Dalai Lama and spiritual leader of the Tibetan Buddhist people.

THE TRAIN RIDE from Delhi to Dharamsala in northern India took about eight hours. I slept for three of those hours, and spent several more talking with members of the delegation, especially Aminul Haque, the Bengali minister of posts and telecommunications, who had brought his bright and very inquisitive teenage son with him. The three of us talked about our new findings in the Qur'an and the Injil, of course, and much else, and the friendship we forged lasts to this day.

For the rest of the ride, I gazed out at the passing countryside and its endless ocean of poverty-stricken humanity, thinking about the history behind the community we were going to visit.

In the 1950s, the People's Republic of China put down a widespread rebellion in Tibet with a vehemence that led to the massive slaughter and displacement of tens of thousands of Tibetans. (According to Tibetan exiles, the number of Tibetans killed by the Chinese totals over 1.2 million, a figure China hotly contests.) A systematic effort to purge the country of its spiritual heritage resulted in the destruction of thousands of Buddhist temples, leaving only a handful intact.

In 1959, the current Dalai Lama was forced to flee Tibet and was granted asylum by India's prime minister, Jawaharlal Nehru. He has lived in Dharamsala ever since.

North of Dharamsala, India is separated from Tibet by the forbidding Himalayan mountain range, the most impenetrable mountain system on the planet and home to the world's fourteen tallest mountains. Over the half-century since the Dalai Lama took refuge in Dharamsala, thousands of Tibetans have braved the Himalayas to settle in the growing community of Tibetan exiles. Many perished in the attempt.

Another Green Line, I thought as I gazed out my train window at the distant peaks.

AFTER WE ARRIVED, we drove for a good three hours up a series of steep, winding roads with massive cliffs dropping off just outside our vehicle's windows and large trucks whizzing past us around the corners. It seemed a miracle to me that we made it the entire way without a head-on collision.

We finally reached our destination, an incredibly ornate Tibetan Buddhist enclave. That night, we had a delicious dinner and then settled into our rooms. The next day we went into the palace for an audience with His Holiness.

There is a certain protocol to meetings with the Dalai Lama. It is considered disrespectful to look him in the eye, and while it is allowable to come near him, touching him is considered a grave infraction. The phrase "His Holiness" is not merely a title; he is considered holy indeed, the literal reincarnation of Avalokitesvara, the bodhisattva of compassion, in a lineage of incarnations dating back to the fourteenth century. To the Tibetans, he doesn't simply *represent* holiness: he *is* holiness.

There were about ten of us in the group: members of parliament from Nepal, Bangladesh, India, and a few other countries, and me. As head of the delegation, I was seated next to the Dalai Lama himself.

As we conversed, the subject of China came up. Turning toward him, though careful not to look directly at him, I asked, "How does your heart feel toward the Chinese? They massacred a million or more of your people, forced you into exile, and have driven huge numbers of your people over the Himalayan mountains to seek refuge. Do you harbor ill feelings toward them?"

His Holiness said, "No, I've forgiven them."

"You know," I mused, "you sound like you're speaking about the teachings of Jesus."

He replied, "Not only am I talking about the teachings of Jesus, but I try to adhere to the teachings of Jesus. I love Jesus. And I'm not worthy to untie his sandals." This was a direct quotation from Jesus's cousin John (the Baptist), who when asked whether he was the Messiah said:

One is coming after me, who is greater than I, the strings of whose shoes I am not worthy to untie. (Luke 3:16)

A little surprised to hear the Gospel being quoted by this Buddhist spiritual leader, I said, "So you've read the scriptures."

"Yes," he replied, "I read the scriptures quite a bit."

"Your Holiness," I said, "this is not a religious group. If it were, we would be all Christians, or all Buddhists, or all Muslims. But we come as a diverse group from every calling, a group formed around the teachings of Jesus, the very things you speak of." I couldn't help looking him right in the eye as we spoke, and he looked directly back at me.

Immediately his aides came around from behind our chairs, fretting and gesticulating, protesting, "Your Holiness! Your Holiness!" and trying to put their hands between us to cut off the contact. But His Holiness swatted at them like they were flies, saying, "Sst! Get away! Sst! Shoo!" The aides bowed down and backed away from us, their eyes downcast. As is accurately depicted in the film *Seven Years in Tibet*, people are not permitted to look directly into the eyes of His Holiness.

We kept talking like that, face-to-face, for another forty or fifty minutes, perhaps longer. I lost track of time. We talked about Jesus, about the power of his teachings and how they are not about being "Christian" or about any religion, but about people's hearts being changed by a divine love moving through them. We talked about the experience of being human, about forgiveness and reconciliation, about the things that drive us apart and the things that bring us together.

Suddenly he said, "Let's take a photograph"—and before I could react, he grabbed my hand.

His aides freaked out. "*Your Holiness! Your Holiness!*" They scrambled up and tried to knock our hands apart—not touching him, of course, but grabbing my arms and pulling on me. Again, His Holiness swatted at his aides, using one hand to shoo them away while gripping my hand with the other. He then rose to his feet and we all stood with him, and with him still holding onto my hand, we all walked outside and down the palace steps. His aides followed, looking desperate.

We stopped at the bottom of the steps, where we had our photograph taken. He was still holding my hand. I turned to him and said, "Your Holiness, I'm going to tell you, in the spirit of the Jesus whom you talked about and whom you love, I love you."

And Tenzin Gyatso, the fourteenth Dalai Lama, reached over and wrapped me in a great big bear hug.

"Your HOLINESS!" His aides fell to the ground, for all the world like they were going to have seizures right then and there on the palace grounds. Looking at him and touching his hand was bad enough—but the hug was just too much for them.

We bid our farewells and left. I never saw the aides get up; for all I know, they could be there still, face down on the stone walkway, still mortified that His Holiness gave the strange American a hug.

TWELVE

Jesus, the Ruhallah

After leaving India, I thought a good deal about my experiences at the conference in Agra and my encounter with the Dalai Lama, but I thought even more about my time with someone else on that trip. There was something that still nagged at me.

After leaving Dharamsala, as we traveled south again to Delhi where we would divide and go our separate ways, I had another conversation with my new friend Aminul Haque, the Bengali cabinet member. In that conversation we reached what I had by now come to think of as "the inevitable *yes, but.*"

Every time I spoke with anyone at length about my findings in the Bible and the Qur'an, regardless of whether the people I spoke with were Christian or Muslim, I inevitably got the same response. The other person would be skeptical or downright incredulous at first, then listen, then be stunned and amazed and say, "This is revolutionary!"

However, if the conversation continued long enough, they would invariably come to the point where they'd say, "Yes— *but . . .*"

And the "but" was always about Jesus.

"This is the thing," Aminul explained. "Christians say he was divine, that he was the only begotten son of God, and that he died on the cross. For a Muslim, every one of these ideas is heretical and blasphemous. They are simply impossible to entertain. I'm sorry, but this is something we just can't get past."

I had heard the same words many times before from Christians and Muslims alike: "There's no way past this barrier. We can never believe what they believe."

I needed to find out once and for all if this was really so.

ONE EVENING IN late 1999, just a few days before the beginning of the new millennium, I sat at home with the Qur'an on one knee and the Bible on the other, struggling with the issue of Jesus's identity as the Son of God. I had to admit, it did seem like a point of contention that absolutely would not budge.

The Qur'an describes Jesus in the most exalted terms, referring to him as "the Messiah" more than ten times, the "Word of Allah," and even suggesting that he was supernaturally conceived. But when it comes to suggesting that he was the "begotten son of God," that's where Muslims draw the line.

In fact, it's not hard to imagine that the Jewish contemporaries of Paul, James, and Peter would have felt exactly the same way. In Greek and Roman mythology, the gods routinely had sexual intercourse with human women. To them, this was not a shocking or unusual idea at all. For example, among the famed collection of Gianlorenzo Bernini's statuary art at the Borghese Gallery in Rome, the most spectacular examples are the sculptures of gods raping women. Likewise, in Hindu mythology, sexual congress between gods and human women is an everyday affair. But to first-century Jews or seventh-century Muslims, this would have been an absolutely abhorrent idea—as it is to Muslims today.

To a Muslim, the idea of Allah fathering a child is not only heresy and blasphemy, it's downright disgusting. "Begetting" is an animal act. The majesty of Allah, having carnal relations with a human female? Perish the thought!

In *aya* after *aya* (twenty-three times, to be exact), the Qur'an makes it emphatically clear that Allah does not, has not, and could not "beget" a child.

He begetteth not, nor is He begotten. (sura 112:3)

For it is not consonant with the majesty of (Allah) Most Gracious that He should beget a son. (sura 19:92)

In fact, this issue is so severe that many Muslims refuse even to open the pages of the Injil or any part of the Bible, for fear that they might accidentally read aloud the phrase "Son of God" and so condemn themselves to a cursed existence.

To a Christian, the issue is just as nonnegotiable. After all, this belief cuts to the very core of the Christian Apostles' Creed:

I believe in Jesus Christ, the only begotten Son of God, our Lord, who was conceived by the Holy Spirit, born of the virgin Mary.

"The only begotten Son of God": right there, as far as Muslims are concerned, the discussion is over.

The New Testament states clearly, at least fifteen times, that Jesus *was* begotten. The Qur'an states unequivocally, at least eleven times, that Isa was *not* begotten. "This feels more intractable than the toughest cease-fire negotiation," I muttered—and the frustrating aptness of the simile was not lost on me.

I closed my Qur'an, glanced at my open copy of the Aramaic Peshitta, and then closed it as well, discouraged. Maybe my Bengali friend was right. *I'm sorry, but this is something we just can't get past.*

It seemed like a dead end.

Almost absentmindedly, I ambled over to my desk and reached into one of the bookshelves behind it. I picked out my

Hebrew Old Testament, set it on my lap, and began to flip aimlessly through the pages. Sometimes, when dealing with an irreducible problem between A and B, it's soothing to put both parties out of mind and turn one's attention to C.

Flipping past Genesis, Exodus, Leviticus, and the rest of the Torah, my fingers continued on past the Nevi'im (Prophets) and stopped at the Psalms. I turned a single page and found myself gazing at Psalm 2, one of the famous "prophetic Psalms" that refer to a future Messiah. The seventh verse is particularly well known to Christians, since it is quoted or clearly alluded to in all four Gospel accounts: "You are my son; this day have I begotten you" (Ps. 2:6).

There it was, right there in the original Hebrew, that theological thorn in the side of East-West relations for centuries. *Today I have begotten you.*

I glanced at the Hebrew word that our English versions translate as "begotten."

Y'lidti-cha.

Turning back to my bookshelf, I pulled out my *Strong's Concordance* and looked up the word. There it was, #3205 in the Hebrew dictionary section of *Strong's: yâlad,* a verb in the *Qal* stem.[1] Reading on, I learned that this is a word of feminine gender: it denotes a *mother giving birth.*

I thought this was curious. A mother? Not a father?

In English, we have hardly any distinctions between masculine and feminine words (other than the indefinite third-person pronoun, "he/she" or "his/her"), and verbs have no gender. Because of this, it's sometimes difficult for English-speaking people to fully grasp the significance of gender in language. But in many tongues, even such familiar ones as French and Spanish, it's a major distinction. In the Semitic languages, it's huge— especially when it comes to the lexicon of reproduction.

Hebrew has other terms that could have been used for the idea of "begotten." For example, the masculine stem *holid,* which would describe a father generating offspring. That term is used freely throughout the Hebrew Bible—but not in this passage. Here the feminine form of the word is applied, even though there is no "mother" or female person referred to anywhere in the sentence—or indeed, in the entire psalm.

Why?

I felt my pulse quicken.

Was the implication here that there was no male act involved in the "begetting," that is, no sexual impregnation? I hastily retrieved my Peshitta and turned to the Gospel account of Matthew.

Just as in Hebrew, in Aramaic there are two distinct terms for the idea of "causing to be born": the masculine *yalad*, which describes the male act of sexual congress and impregnation, and the feminine passive *ettled*, which refers to the female act of conceiving, gestating, and delivering an offspring. In the Greek, both are translated with the same genderless term, *gennao*, from which we derive "generate" and "generation."

And it is the matter of *generation* with which the New Testament begins. The Gospel of Matthew opens with an extensive genealogy of Jesus, listing who was begotten by whom from Abraham all the way to Joseph, the husband of Mary (Matt. 1:1–16). In the Aramaic version, this entire chronology uses the term *yalad* or *awled*, a male stem meaning "from him" and suggesting regeneration through sexual intercourse—until the very last step in the genealogical sequence, when it suddenly changes terms:

> Jacob begot [*awled*] Joseph the husband of Mary, of whom was born [*ettled*] Jesus. (Matt. 1:16)

After progressing through thirty-eight generations, each one of them described with the word *yalad* or *awled*, for this very last generation the text switches to the word *ettled*, a female stem meaning "from her"—implying that there was no "him" to cite in this last generation.

What about other Injil verses dealing with Isa being "begot-ten"? I eagerly flipped the pages and found one of the most famous verses in the New Testament, John 3:16:

> For God so loved the world that he even gave his only be-gotten [*yachidaya*] Son, so that whoever believes in him should not perish, but have eternal life.

The Aramaic word used here, *yachidaya*, is rooted in the Semitic word for "oneness," "alone," or "unique." And I was pretty sure that the very same word was used in its Hebrew form, *ykhiaday*, in a prophetic verse in—and now I switched back to my Hebrew Bible to confirm—yes, there it was, in Zechariah:

> They shall look upon me whom they have pierced, and they shall mourn for him as they mourn for an *only son* [*ykhiaday*]. (Zech. 12:10)

This word has a meaning quite different from that of the other, male forms of "begotten." It is often applied to an orphan, a fa-therless son or firstborn heir.[2]

Could it be that, once again, there was a linguistic misunder-standing at the core of this conflict? It seemed that all three Semitic languages were saying the same thing: the Messiah/Jesus/Isa was *not* conceived through a male act of sexual con-gress but *was* conceived uniquely and through a specifically and exclusively female process.

As strange as this sounds—God conceiving a child through an "exclusively female" process?—it made perfect sense.

Both the Qur'an and Gospel accounts describe the announce-ment of Jesus's conception and birth the same way: the angel Gabriel comes to a virgin named Mary and tells her that God will conceive a son within her. Mary, not surprisingly, is startled by this news. As Luke's Gospel account reports it:

Then Mary said to the angel, How can this be, for no man has known me. The angel answered and said to her, The Holy Spirit [Aramaic: *Rohka Alaha*] will come, and the power of the Highest will rest upon you; therefore, the one who is to be born of you is holy, and he will be called the Son of God. (Luke 1:34–35)

Here is how the Qur'an describes the same scene:

She [Mary] said: "O my Lord! How shall I have a son when no man hath touched me?" He said, "Even so; Allah createth what He willeth: when He hath decreed a plan, He but saith to it, 'Be' and it is [Arabic: *kun faya kun*]!" (sura 3:47)

This last is a very important concept in Islam. The Arabic *kun faya kun* ("'Be!' and it is") describes the way Allah causes things to occur simply by his command. This is identical to the way the Torah describes the Creation: at each stage of the creation process, God causes things to come into being simply by uttering the command. Our English rendering, "And God said 'Let there be light'; and there was light," does not fully convey the feeling of the passage, the sense that God was not simply narrating an event (like Charlton Heston in a Hollywood film) but was issuing a direct, generative command to the elements. Dr. Pat Mercer Hutchens, a Hebrew scholar, told me that a more accurate translation of the Hebrew would be something like this: "Elohim spoke, 'Light—*Be!*' And light *was*."

I looked at the first page of Genesis in my Hebrew Torah and noticed something else: in the passage just before the creation of light, it describes the condition that immediately preceded creation:

And the spirit of God moved upon the face of the waters. (Gen. 1:2)

Interestingly, the Hebrew word *ruach* (spirit) is used here in its feminine form. The "moving upon" of God's spirit (*ruach elohem*) just prior to God's creation by fiat is strikingly reminiscent of how Gabriel describes the coming event to Mary: that the Holy Spirit will "overshadow" her and thus a new life will be created—as the Qur'an says, *kun faya kun*, purely by God's command.

Here is how Matthew's Gospel describes the conception:

> The birth of Jesus Christ was in this manner. While Mary his mother was acquired for a price for Joseph, before they came together, she was found with child of the Holy Spirit [Aramaic: *Rohka Alaha*]. (Matt. 1:18)

And again, from the Qur'an:

> We breathed into her of our Spirit [Arabic: *Ruhina,* commonly referred to in Islam as Ruhallah, "Spirit of God"] and We made her and her son a sign for all peoples. (suras 21:91 and 66:12)

It seems clear that both the Gospel accounts and the Qur'anic verses describe Jesus's conception identically: as a spiritually generated conception. There is no sexual contact, not with Joseph and certainly not with God or Allah. Just as at the very beginning of the Creation, when the *ruach elohem* hovered over the face of the waters and God commanded light into being, the *rohka alaha* now hovers over the young Mary as God generates the conception of a child purely through the *kun faya kun* power of his command.

Could it really be this simple? Or was this wishful thinking on my part? Had I missed some critical flaw in the logic? I checked it all again, every verse, *aya,* and word. No mistake. There was no ambiguity in the matter. The different traditions describe precisely the same event: Jesus was *not* "begotten" in the usual fashion but was conceived supernaturally by a command of Allah/God.

Which brought me to the second major Christological stumbling block: the issue of the deity of Jesus. For this I would have to wait; it was late, and I had a busy day beginning early in the morning. With dozens of bookmarks in place, I set the precious texts aside and headed for bed, wondering how I would ever be able to sleep.

DURING A WHIRLWIND trip to Bangladesh, I once had the privilege of sitting at dinner with two dozen top scholars in the capital city of Dhaka. Bangladesh is a strongly Muslim country; in fact, it is the third-largest Muslim-majority country in the world (after Indonesia and Pakistan).

As we became better acquainted over our meal, I asked this distinguished group what they thought of Isa al-Masih. Their answer came unanimously, like a beautiful chorus: "Isa! Ahhhh, *Ruhallah! Ruhallah!* [Spirit of God!]"

I was amazed. I had not suggested this or even uttered the phrase. Their response was immediate and spontaneous. To this devout group of educated Muslims, Jesus *is* the Qur'anic *Ruhallah*—the spirit of Allah.

Yet still, the suggestion that Jesus holds any aspect of deity is perhaps the single most critical issue dividing Islam and Christianity.

It was days before I could resume my study, and when I did I had brought out a stack of historical references from my library. I suspected that the answers I sought would not be found purely within the Rosetta stone of Semitic linguistics, but would require taking a long view of human affairs as well.

This controversy was not born with the advent of Islam in the seventh century: people had been debating the nature of Jesus ever since the days of his earthly ministry. In the early fourth century, the emperor Constantine convened a group of several hundred in Nicaea, the first of a long series of Ecumenical Councils, to try to resolve the issue once and for all.

At one point the raging debate boiled down to a disagreement between two words—actually, to be more precise, between *two letters* in a word. One group wanted to describe Jesus as *homoiousious*, "of a *similar* substance" to God, while another insisted that he be described as *homoousious*, "of the *same* substance" as God. Constantine came down on the side of the homoousians, and thus today we have the Nicene Creed, which declares that Jesus is "begotten, not made, being *of one substance* with the Father."

But imperial edict or not, it was an issue that just wouldn't die. A second council followed in 381, a third in 431, a fourth in 451— and in the year 681, half a century *after* the death of Muhammad, the seventh Ecumenical Council was *still* dealing with the debate around the divine versus human nature of Jesus.

But with the Semitic texts of the holy books spread before me, I didn't think we needed to get into theological hair-splitting to resolve this issue. The plain truth is, most of the faithful on either side of the fence would agree that the flesh and body of the man Jesus was physical, finite, and distinctly human. I also thought both sides would agree that his spirit was quite another story.

It seemed to me that the discoveries I had made a few weeks earlier, about the issue of whether or not Jesus was "begotten," nicely addressed the issue of his divinity as well.

The masculine and feminine verb forms of the Semitic languages confirm what common logic would conclude from both the Gospel and Qur'anic accounts: Jesus/Isa was conceived by a purely energetic act of spirit, a conception sparked within Mary without benefit of sexual act. Once conceived, he implanted and gestated in the normal fashion, meaning that the material that formed his body was provided through his human mother. He was born normally, physically, as a human being, with the uniquely different point that half his DNA was contributed not by a male sperm from a human father but by a spiritual source.

In the simpler language of the Qur'an, the *Ruhallah* supernaturally conceived Isa in the womb of a virgin, and that same *Ruhallah* resided within him throughout his life. Thus, it made perfect sense that when I asked a roomful of Muslim scholars about Jesus, they responded, *Ruhallah! Ruhallah!*

It was no wonder, I thought, that so many have struggled with this issue for so many centuries. The question of Jesus's nature is an utterly unique situation within our collective historical experience, and one that does not have a simple, clearcut, yes-or-no answer. Is Jesus an ordinary flesh-and-blood human being? *Yes and no.* Does Isa have a divine nature? *Yes and no.* Or perhaps it's more accurate to put it this way: Is Jesus/Isa made of flesh and blood like the rest of us, or is he animated by the Spirit of God? *Yes . . . and yes.*

And on these points, although they don't seem to realize it, Christianity and Islam agree.

BUT WHAT ABOUT this vexing issue of the Trinity? The phrase "Father, Son, and Holy Spirit" has been at the center of seemingly intractable disagreements and conflicts both within the Christian community and between the Christian and Muslim communities for centuries. Here is what the Qur'an has to say on the matter:

And say not "Trinity": desist: it will be better for you: for Allah is one God. (sura 4:171)

They do blaspheme who say Allah is one of the three in a Trinity; for there is no god except One God. (sura 5:73)

But is this a genuine conflict, or could it once again be simply an issue of linguistic semantics?

Throughout the Qur'an (and at times in the Torah, such as in Genesis 1), verses where Allah is speaking in the first person are written in the plural and often translated into English as "we." This is a typical Semitic way of honoring God, as he is too majestic to be referred to in the singular. No Muslim views God as being literally a plurality, but his many attributes are of such great importance that his very nature can only be described in plural terms.

The Qur'an ascribes as many as ninety-nine different names or *sifat* (divine attributes) to Allah: Allah's word, Allah's power, Allah's life, Allah's mercy, compassion, knowledge, and so on. A list of these *sifat*, incidentally, forms a remarkably close parallel to the New Testament portrayal of Alaha and his attributes.

Eastern Orthodox Christians, who subscribe to some but not all of the Ecumenical Councils, say they believe in one God with *three attributes* rather than with *three persons*. Those of the Nestorian sect also preferred the Aramaic word for "attributes" (*kenomey*) to the Greek concept of "persons" (*prosopon*).

Though I have great respect for the idea, the term "trinity" is nowhere to be found in the Bible. In fact, the specific Christian doctrine of "One God, Three Persons" was not adopted until after the First Council of Nicaea in 325. The biblical verse that perhaps comes closest to the trinity idea is the so-called tri-unity phrase in the first Letter of John:

> For there are three that bear witness in heaven: the Father, the Word, and the Holy Spirit; and these three are one. (1 John 5:7, NKJV)[3]

Interestingly, the writer refers here not to a "son" but to the "Word," which refers to the Messiah, Jesus. John's Gospel, of course, also famously speaks about Jesus as the Word of God, even to the point of opening with a passage that is deliberately set in parallel to the opening of Genesis:

> In the beginning was the Word, and the Word was with God, and the Word was God.

The "Word of God," *Kalimat Allah,* is also one of many attributes that the Qur'an ascribes to Isa (suras 3:39, 3:45, and 4:171). It also mentions the Holy Spirit twenty-four times.

The Qur'an gives ninety-nine attributes of God; the Bible ascribes forty-six attributes to God and twenty-four specific names (El-Shaddai or "God who provides all," Jehovah-Tsidkenu or "God our provider," Jehovah-Rohi or "The Lord our shepherd," Elohim, El-Elyon, etc.). The attributes of "Father," "Holy Spirit," and "Son" or "Word" are primal in the Christian tradition, but whether you call them "persons" or "attributes," the meaning is the same: we are all talking about a single God, albeit one with many aspects.

All three holy books (Torah, New Testament, and Qur'an) describe these three same entities or attributes of Deity—God, Holy Spirit, and Messiah. I have asked distinguished clerics, both Muslim and Christian, if they could explain to me the interaction of these three deified attributes, and after much bantering back and forth, in the end they have all given me the exact same answer: "Mark, it's a mystery." So what are we arguing about?

As far as I could see, the controversy around the concept of the trinity was a theological red herring. Neither Christians nor Jews believe in a pantheon of multiple gods any more than Muslims do (or the monotheistic Sikhs, for that matter).

WHICH BROUGHT ME to the third and final major Christological stumbling block: the Crucifixion. And this was an issue, I knew, that would take serious study. An early Muslim writer described the possible consequences of this controversy in a vivid account:

> Al-Uris saw in a deep sleep Christ Jesus, son of Mary, who seemed to turn his face toward him from heaven. He asked him: "Did the crucifixion really happen?" Jesus said, "Yes." Al-Uris then relayed his dream to an interpreter, who said, "The man who saw this dream shall be crucified. For Jesus is infallible and can only speak the truth . . . because the Glorious Qur'an specifically states that Jesus was not crucified or killed. Accordingly, this must refer to the dreamer— and it is he who shall be crucified." This matter turned out as the interpreter said.[4]

The Crucifixion of Jesus is one of the most serious bones of contention between Islam and Christianity. Poor Al-Uris was himself crucified in the seventh century for even dreaming of such a blasphemous event.

Why blasphemous? Ask any Muslim and he'll tell you, "Because the Qur'an says it didn't happen." Yet of the more than 6,600 *ayas* in the Qur'an, the assertion that Jesus was *not* crucified derives from a single passage, and it was here that my investigation began:

> They said (in boast), "We killed Christ Jesus the son of Mary, the Messenger of Allah"—but they killed him not, nor crucified him. But so it was made to appear to them [Arabic: *shubbiha la-hum*] . . . for of a surety they killed him not. (sura 4:157)

This is a fascinating verse. The "they" in question here is a reference to the Jews; sura 4:153–156 is a discussion of a group of Jewish people, which continues into this verse. Though it's hard to imagine this from our twenty-first-century vantage point, there were then certain Jewish groups—both in Jesus's own time and six centuries later in the prophet Muhammad's time—who actively sought credit for the capital punishment of Jesus. The Qur'anic passage clearly alludes to this, most likely speaking of certain Jews in Medina, when it points out that these particular Jews said *in boast* that they had killed Jesus.

But boast or not, the historical facts are otherwise, as the Qur'an itself points out. Both the Gospel accounts and references in contemporary secular histories confirm that the controversial young rabbi from Nazareth was sentenced to death and executed by the Roman authorities in Jerusalem. Indeed, it couldn't have been otherwise: only the Romans had the legal authority to do so.

The Qur'anic record appears to be saying, in essence: "Even if a few of them claim credit, it was absolutely not the Jews who killed or crucified Jesus."

Then there is the curiously ambiguous phrase, ". . . but so it was made to appear to them." What on earth does that mean? Good question—and as it turns out, there is no single agreed-upon answer. In the year 923, some three centuries after the Qur'an was first written down, the Arabic scholar al-Tabari suggested four possible answers to this perplexing question:

1. Jesus did not die on the cross but was only made unconscious;

2. It was not Jesus on the cross; someone else was crucified in his place;

3. Jesus did in fact die, but not on the cross; in other words, he was miraculously saved from the cross and not killed at all, but died later by other means (by implication, of natural or at least nonviolent causes) and was subsequently taken up to Allah;

4. Jesus did in fact die on the cross, just as the "people of the Book" (Christians) claim.

The second option, that someone else was crucified in Jesus's place, has been bandied about for centuries, and certainly would fit that odd phrase *shubbiha la-hum* ("so it was made to appear to them"). Muslim tradition in some circles has held that Jesus's likeness was somehow transferred onto Judas Iscariot's body, or that someone who looked similar to Jesus was hoisted onto the cross instead, in some sort of morbid hoax.

Yet another interpretation, held by some Sufi (Muslim) mystics and certain Christian sects (the Nestorians again), was that it was only Jesus's physical, human form that was crucified on the cross, while his aspect as spirit was received by Allah into heaven, and that the Qur'an meant only to deny the death of the Spirit.

Whatever the truth may be, the meaning of the phrase is not clear and is still a matter of debate today. But one thing does seem abundantly clear: the passage is not a categorical denial that Jesus died on the cross, it simply denies that the Jews were responsible for the execution. In fact, the Qur'an itself speaks directly and repeatedly of the death of Jesus. In sura 19:33, Jesus says, "So peace is on me the day I was born, the day that I die [Arabic: *amutu*],[5] and the day that I shall be raised up to life (again)."[6] Sura 5:117 reiterates this by having Jesus say, "When Thou didst take me [cause me to die] [Arabic: *tawaffaytani*]."[7]

Then why the controversy? If the most one can really conclude from this passage is that it is confusing at best, and if both the historical record and the Gospel accounts—which the Qur'an repeatedly urges us to hold in the highest regard—record that this event did indeed occur, then why the emphatic insistence on the part of Islamic tradition and dogma that Jesus did *not* die on the cross?

Perhaps another answer here lay not in the study of linguistics but in the more subjective matter of human experience over the generations since the Qur'an first appeared. To understand what the cross has come to mean to Muslims, it is necessary to appreciate what happened during the Crusades.

During the first several centuries of Islam, the prevalent picture of Isa within Muslim culture was quite different from what
it would soon become. He was a figure of supreme relevance
and affinity. And in Sufi tradition Isa was quite similar to the
figure of the Gospels.

The extreme and widespread violence that spanned the two
centuries from the late eleventh century to the late thirteenth
century profoundly changed things. Whether Jesus was crucified had been a matter of debate since the inception of Islam; the
Crusades solidified the issue. During this horrific killing spree,
many thousands of Muslims were raped and murdered by ma-
rauding Western armies—who were clothed with symbolic crosses
splashed across their chests, shields, and helmets. Indeed, their
very killing instruments (their swords) were shaped like crosses.
In the course of their campaign, they demanded that their pris-
oners convert, a process that included the confession that Jesus
was nailed to a cross.

Is it any surprise that Islam, in an effort to protect its way of
life and even its very survival, would reject the symbol of the
cross and all it had come to stand for?

As I BEGAN putting away my books, I thought about the issue
of Jesus's death, and the centuries of bitter dispute, bias, preju-
dice, and persecution that have raged around this event. *Our
history lies behind us,* I thought; *it's high time we began putting these
historic biases and divisions behind us as well.*

It occurred to me that the very passage that has been used as
an instrument of division for centuries also has a tremendous
potential for cultural healing. For those of us seeking common
ground, it provides official Qur'anic affirmation that it was *not*
Jews who put Jesus to death.

Even today, "Christ-killer" is an epithet still hurled at Jews, and
by more people than one might think. In 2003, an Associated Press

poll found that more than *one in four* people believed that the Jews were responsible for Jesus's death.

The truth, of course, is quite the opposite. Not only was Jesus Jewish himself; it was also a generation of Jews—Peter, Paul, John, James, and their colleagues—who first recognized his teachings for the revolutionary movement they were and who anchored that movement in Jerusalem, Turkey, and Rome and laid the foundation for it to spread throughout the world.

Ironically, the people who actually performed the trial, conviction, sentencing, and execution were the forebears not of today's Jews but of today's Italians—a people who have over the centuries been among the most committed, devout followers of the carpenter from Galilee. Does anyone seriously think we should label Italians "Christ-killers"? The very idea is ludicrous.

What makes it even more so is the fact, clear as day in the Bible and solidly established as Christian doctrine, that far from resisting or struggling to avoid death, Jesus himself did virtually everything he could to *invite* the process of arrest, conviction, and execution. He even says this explicitly: "I lay down my life so that I may take it up again. No man takes it away from me, but I lay it down of my own will" (John 10:17–18).

Which brings us to the truly tragic absurdity of the "Christ-killer" label and the blame game that has dogged the Gospel accounts for over two thousand years. Jesus himself, breathing out his last on the cross, put it this way: "Father, forgive them, for they know not what they do." How ridiculous is it for us to be carrying around a grudge two thousand years later, when the victim himself had already let it go before the crime was even completed?

So it wasn't Jews, it was Romans. Does it matter? Regardless of who they were or what group they belonged to, the truth is exactly as he put it: they knew not what they were doing.

I thought of the hundreds of thousands killed in the Crusades, the Inquisition, and pogroms; of the millions of victims of genocides in the last century alone, in Armenia, Afghanistan, Russia,

China, Tibet. I thought of Sabra and Shatilla, Treblinka and Ausch-witz, Cambodia and Rwanda. From the most power-mad despot atop the chain of destruction down to the blindly raging foot soldier carrying out his carnage-causing commands, *they knew not what they were doing.*

I thought of the people in our own ordinary lives whom we hurt through neglect or little cruelties, intentional or not, even sometimes those closest to us. Which among us, I thought, has not caused pain and suffering to others?

For centuries our cultures have been kept apart by our ac-counts of what happened or did not happen to Jesus on the cross. Perhaps it's time we let ourselves be brought together by what he *said* on the cross.

Father, forgive them, for they know not what they do.

To which among us do those words not apply?

As the months and seasons wore on, I continued to travel everywhere I could and to talk with whomever I could, engag-ing in dialogue and discussion about these findings. More than ever, I was convinced that there was tremendously fertile ground for reconciliation between East and West, and that the person and the teachings of Jesus—not the religious or theological claims about him—were key to this process.

Finally, after one especially busy summer of travels, I man-aged to find a little time to return to the Himalayas with my wife, Nancy. I had long wanted to bring her on a quiet trip to Nepal, a favorite place of mine and one of the most beautiful in the world. We hadn't had a vacation in ages.

On the way, our plane stopped over in London, and I picked up a newspaper at Heathrow. In it I read a story about how two American aid workers in Afghanistan had been arrested by the Taliban, how they stood accused of "preaching Christianity" and might get the death penalty. The story quoted a Taliban foreign minister as saying, "Jesus is highly regarded here, but Christianity is not."

It saddened me to think of how much division, pain, and suffering has been created around the world's religious distinctions, about how the movements inspired by such men as Abraham, Moses, Jesus, and Muhammad have been converted, one by one, into fuel for ever more vicious Green Lines that keep us apart.

At the same time, I was strongly inspired by the first half of the foreign minister's statement: "Jesus is highly regarded here." It reminded me of a story I heard about Mahatma Gandhi.

A group of Christian leaders listened intently to an impassioned speech by Gandhi and afterward commented that they were shocked at how much of what he had said sounded very much like the teachings of Jesus. Why, they asked him, was he not a Christian himself?

Gandhi replied, "If Christians acted more like Jesus, then I would be one."

Maybe, I thought, *it's possible that millions of Christians will start doing exactly that.*

Nancy and I boarded our plane and headed off to Nepal, where we anticipated a full week of glorious relaxation. As we flew, I thought eagerly about the possibilities for rapprochement, reconciliation, and peace. I looked forward to our week of rest in Nepal and to whatever work might be in store for us upon our return. I didn't know what lay ahead, but felt sure there would be rich opportunities for bringing the world community together and helping it to heal its wounds. I felt hopeful, even optimistic about the future.

Glancing again at my newspaper, I happened to note the date above the headlines. It was September 10, 2001.

To Walk in Another Man's Sandals

We got the news over dinner in Kathmandu. Because of the time difference, it was about 6:30 in the evening for us when reports came in over our Nepali dinner hosts' cell phones that a plane had crashed into the North Tower of the World Trade Center and the building had burst into flames. We could hardly believe it was true. "Some Piper Cub must have gone off course out of Newark or JFK," I murmured to Nancy, "but how on earth could it be so off-course as to fly straight into . . ." My voice trailed off, not even wanting to finish the thought or follow its implications.

Minutes later the cell phones began ringing again and we heard a second report: another plane had hit the South Tower. I knew instantly what this meant. Malcolm Kalp's worst nightmare was now our waking reality. I grabbed my cell phone and called one of my staff back in the States.

"I don't know how long we can stay on the phone," he said, "the lines in D.C. and New York are totally jammed. The whole country's under attack. The Pentagon's been hit, the White

House may be next. There are planes hitting all over the place!"—and then we lost our phone connection.

Nancy and I hastily finished our dinner and went back to our hotel room. It was supposed to be a romantic interlude in a gorgeous, exotic locale. And it was indeed beautiful—but, as it turned out, not so romantic. The two of us spent that night and all the next day glued to CNN, weeping.

The image that most seared itself into my heart was a shot of Manhattan taken from the Jersey side, showing a great mass of smoke slowly pouring up and outward to form a vast cloud that hung over the city. The cloud did not dissipate for weeks.

We did make it to India a few days later. Everywhere we went, the local people were quite downcast. "This is going to change everything," one man said, giving voice to the thoughts we saw in everyone's eyes. "The whole world's going to be different now."

He was right. When we returned home a week later, it was as if we had come back to a different country. Despite the lengthy, agonizingly frustrating ordeal of the Iran hostages; despite the horrors of the Beirut marine barracks bombing and litany of terrorist attacks ever since; despite the clear and growing danger of militant Muslim extremism, Americans on the whole had still felt largely immune. Now the reality had struck home, and the nation—and to some extent the entire world—was profoundly shaken.

IN THE AFTERMATH of 9/11, Congress was like a ghost town. Capitol Hill is normally home to a constant, hectic flow of traffic, jammed with a hundred senators, over four hundred congressmen, and their thousands of staff. But in the weeks and months following the September attacks, most were so nervous about being killed, whether by anthrax or another suicide bombing, that people stayed home in droves.

Being a former congressman allows me to come and go on Capitol Hill and use the congressional dining room at will. In the nearly fifteen years since leaving office, I had often used that privilege and had spent countless dozens of hours in that hall in meetings with all sorts of people, from heads of state and other foreign dignitaries to former colleagues from the House. In all those years, I had never seen the place look so desolate.

Throughout the fall of 2001 and into the early months of 2002, I often sat there in complete solitude, sometimes for hours, in a room that comfortably seats a hundred and can manage 135 if you push it. The privately contracted outfit that runs the place was thrilled to have me there. They were going broke running an empty dining hall. "Come back soon—and bring your colleagues and friends!" the staff begged.

During the days immediately following 9/11, I found myself operating with a new level of clarity. There could not be anything more important than the search for new bridges between the East and the West, and I resolved to devote myself fully to this pursuit. What had been in essence a hobby now began to absorb all my time. I needed to make this the focal point of my professional life, I decided, and trust that my family and I would somehow find ways to provide for ourselves.

With a wife, four teenage children, and a fairly large home in a D.C. suburb (where the cost of living is far from the low end of the scale), this was no small proposition. Ever since leaving my official posts in Congress and at the United Nations, I had had to rely largely on my own earnings to finance these trips abroad. A growing network of friends helped make up the difference for trips they felt were especially important, but by and large, the financial burden of these travels fell on me and my family. I often found myself wondering, if I largely abandoned my "day job" and threw myself into the pursuit of these bridges between faiths and cultures, could that network possibly keep up?

But every time my mind became distracted with petty worries about bills and budgets, I felt these thoughts pushed out again by an image I could not shake. I kept seeing that dark gray cloud of ash, debris, and despair hovering over New York. It felt as if I had been seeing that cloud gather for twenty years, from the moment I had sat on a suburban Virginia couch with Malcolm Kalp. And as much as the 9/11 attacks pushed against the boundaries of American imagination, both in the scope of their horror and the extent of their sheer unthinkableness, it seemed certain that unless the course of history were altered and human hearts around the globe influenced to make a profound change, darker clouds than this would gather still.

THE MONTHS IMMEDIATELY following 9/11 were a time of dramatic change for people not only in the United States but throughout the world. For some, it meant a huge escalation of insecurity and fear for the future; for some it was a time of deepening mistrust, resentment, and outright hostility toward other groups. For me, it brought a dramatically different perspective, the beginnings of seeing the Western world through Muslim eyes.

For years now, I had spent many long evenings in Virginia talking and studying with my Muslim friends, Abubaker al-Shingieti and a handful of others. Now my friendships with American Muslims became, to the extent possible, the focus of my every waking moment.

In early October 2001 I went to Chicago at the invitation of a Lebanese American friend who knew quite a few professors at Wheaton College. I had told him about some of our linguistic discoveries in Aramaic and Arabic, and he was excited about them and their implications. As we talked one day about the deepening urgency of taking these findings further, he said, "Why don't you come up here and pass your ideas past the professors here?"

My friend set up meetings for me at the cafeteria at Wheaton, and I had the opportunity to talk with professors of linguistics, comparative religion, Islam, Christianity—by the time we were through it felt as if we had met with the entire faculty. Their reactions were so positive that my friend grew emboldened enough to arrange a meeting with the imam of Chicago, a man named Faisal.

When I shared with Imam Faisal my findings about Jesus, he accusingly said, "You're a con man for Jesus."

I'd never been called *that* before. I suggested that we just keep chatting and see where it might lead. An hour later we were praying together, and his tone had shifted to one of excited receptivity. "If this is all true," he said, "it could be revolutionary. May I come see you in Washington?"

"*Marhaba* [You're welcome to]," I replied, "please do."

"May I bring friends?" he asked.

"*Marhaba*," I repeated, "bring all the friends you want. I'd be happy to receive them."

Imam Faisal was not able to make the trip himself after all, but he did give my name to a friend of his, another imam in Chicago, who called me soon afterward and said he was going to be in the Capitol along with a few other imams from other cities, could we perhaps meet? We made a date to get together at the congressional dining room.

When the day came, I entered the dining room and approached the four Muslim leaders. We all carefully shook hands, introduced ourselves, and took our seats around the table; a brief silence ensued as everyone looked at me. This was less than a month after 9/11 and just a week before the passage of the Patriot Act; President Bush had put the world on notice that we were declaring "war on terror." Muslim Americans were already the target of a sweeping wave of suspicion—at times, of outright hostility. It was clear that these four men weren't sure what kind of meeting they were about to have.

I thanked them for coming and said that I was interested in exploring with them those things we share in common.

One of the men said, "What have you discovered that we have in common?"

"Well," I replied, "what about the sonship of Jesus?"

They stared at me as if I were a man who had completely lost his mind. Many Muslims have told me that the sonship of Jesus—that is, whether or not Jesus is actually the son of God—is the defining issue separating us, and I had opened our conversation by going right to the heart of the matter. If there was going to be any chance at all to share my perspective on this major cultural problem with these learned men, I needed to connect with them and do it fast.

I plunged on. "I know that your own holy book speaks of Jesus in the most unusual ways, and when I say—"

"*Jesus?*"

I was abruptly interrupted by the man sitting next to me. His eyes burned with intensity. This was Abdel, the imam from Chicago whose imam friend Faisal had arranged our meeting.

"Excuse me," said Abdel in his carefully articulated English, "but what Jesus are you talking about?"

I hesitated. I knew that how I answered this question would play a critical part in determining what happened next. My explorations of those controversial issues surrounding the identity and nature of Jesus (what I thought of as the "yes, but" issues) had opened my eyes to the underlying unity and resolution of these issues—but it had also made me acutely aware of how extremely sensitive they were, especially to Muslims of such strong faith as these gentlemen who now faced me, glaring. I looked directly at him and answered in Arabic: "*Ana uru du atakallam ma'ak an Isa ibn Maryam.*"

For a split second Abdel's eyes widened in surprise, and then he visibly relaxed. "Where did you learn that?"

"I have a little knowledge of Arabic," I replied, "not a lot, but some. And I've studied the Qur'an a little bit."

He smiled, ever so slightly. "Ah" was all he said.

"Perhaps," the other man spoke up again, the one who had asked me what I thought we might possibly have in common, "perhaps we have something in common after all."

From that tentative beginning, we began slowly exploring various aspects of our cultures and possible bridges between East and West. After a good hour had passed, my friend Duncan Hunter, who was then chairman of the Armed Services Committee, stopped by our table, thumped me on the back, and said, "Marcus, old friend, who are your guests, and what language are you speaking this time?"

I explained the nature of our meeting. Duncan turned to Abdel and said, "Do you mind if I ask a question?" Abdel nodded for him to go ahead. "What was it I overheard Mark say to you in Arabic, when you all first sat down?"

Abdel replied, "He said, *I want to talk with you about Jesus the son of Mary.*"

"Ah," said Duncan. It was clear from his expression that he was in the dark as to why this would be a significant thing to say, but that out of sensitivity to possible missteps, he was not going to press the question further.

"You see," Abdel explained, "the Jesus of the Bible and the Jesus of the Qur'an are very different. Jesus of the Qur'an is *son of Mary*. In the Qur'an, God is God and Jesus is Jesus: Jesus is not *son of God.*

"We Muslims believe that Christianity as it stands today does not represent the true teachings about Jesus. To us, the West took the name of Jesus and built something around it that was not the real Jesus. In our view, the name Jesus has served as a shield for racism for centuries. To us, the name Jesus stands for the white man, arrogance, colonization, and manipulation.

"If Mark had not said that, if he had just gone on to talk about Jesus, without qualifying who this was he was talking about by saying 'son of Mary,' it would have been a very different meeting. We would have exchanged smiles, shared some breakfast, and left. Nothing would have been accomplished. Instead, I think we may have accomplished very much indeed."

Just like that, in a few simple sentences, Duncan and I had learned more about how the Muslim world views the West, and more about the Muslim experience in the modern world, than a lifetime of formal training would have taught us.

As we got up and walked out of the congressional dining hall together, Abdel said to me, "Mark, we really need to talk more about all this." And so began one of the most powerful and eye-opening friendships of these post-9/11 years.

IN THE DAYS and weeks that followed, Abdel and I talked regularly, and he came to visit often. As with Dr. al-Shingieti and (to a lesser extent) Dr. Treky, the two of us began spending time together sifting through the scriptures and other documents, sharing perspectives on our different traditions and pursuing our study of possible bridges between our cultures. As we got to know each other, I learned more about his background.

Abdel came to the United States from his native Sudan in the eighties to study law. After completing masters and law degrees, he was offered a teaching post in the Chicago area and decided to stay in the States. But the salary from his new teaching position was not enough to support his growing family, so over the years he supplemented his income through a series of modestly successful business ventures. By 2001, he had a small but thriving telecommunications business going, with more than ten thousand customers.

Then 9/11 happened. In the aftermath of the attacks, the wave of suspicion, investigation, and persecution of Arab Americans was so profound that Abdel's customers, virtually all of whom were Arab Americans, were suddenly afraid to have telephone conversations with their friends. For three months, Abdel dug deep into his pockets in a frantic effort to cover his expenses. In mid-December 2001, the end of the month of Ramadan, he finally had to close the business. On top of the crushing psychological and social burdens of discrimination and fear, he took a huge financial loss.

As I soon learned from my growing circle of Muslim friends, Abdel was far from alone: this sort of experience was widespread in the American Muslim community—indeed, in the Muslim community worldwide.

Six weeks after the 9/11 attacks, Congress passed the USA Patriot Act, broadening presidential authority to determine an "extraordinary threat." The FBI began massive audits, raids, and sting operations targeting hundreds of Muslim organizations, including practically every major Muslim or Muslim-related group in the United States.

Designating an organization as "supporter or financer of terrorism," even if this was purely a suspicion with absolutely no evidence behind it, allowed the U.S. Treasury to block or freeze funds belonging to the organization as well as the funds of all individuals involved. The Senate Finance Committee ordered the IRS to turn over the tax returns of nearly two hundred Islamic organizations for review. The Muslim organizations were raided, and everyone engaged with them was systematically investigated. Even when a given group was exonerated, authorities continued investigating the individuals who had donated to that group.

Not surprisingly, contributions quickly dried up; nobody wanted their names on rosters that were being scrutinized. Hundreds of organizations were destroyed, as a thick blanket of paranoia settled like a shadow over the entire Muslim American community. The terrorists had not won a war, but they had clearly won a battle: the events of 9/11 had crippled our nation, not only financially but also emotionally, socially, and spiritually.

Within this climate, my Muslim friends told me, they were taking a significant risk just by talking with me. The possibility, even the likelihood, of being labeled a traitor, perhaps a CIA or FBI plant, was suddenly quite high. The oppressive climate of suspicion spread like a contagion, and it was not confined to the non-Muslim world. As the rest of America became acutely suspicious of Muslims and Arabs everywhere, Muslims soon became suspicious of each other. Some of my friends told me they were coming under a lot of criticism from their own friends because they were speaking with me.

"Some say, 'You're just wasting your time,'" one friend told me, "and that's the nicest of the comments I hear. Some have taken me aside and asked me, how can I be sure this Mark Siljander is not CIA or FBI, trying to entrap me? And I really can't blame them," he continued. "This happens to us all the time. We establish a close relationship with someone in the West, and suddenly we learn that our private details are printed in the *London Times*. For us, 9/11 was as big a shock as it was for everyone else in America. We had no idea that it was coming; it just happened out of nowhere. It was as devastating for us as it was for you. But now we are all considered terrorists and put on watch lists."

ABDEL AND I decided we needed to spend some time together out in the community. It was not enough for me to hear about these experiences from my own limited circle of Muslim friends. If I was going to devote my life to the exploration of bridges between our cultures, it would be important to learn more about the Muslim American experience right in my homeland. And it had to be face-to-face—it had to be *personal*. We decided to take a page from my earliest days in politics and hold some town meetings with the Muslim community.

My first term in public service began when I was just twenty-one and still in graduate school, when I was elected to the office of Fabius Township Trustee in St. Joseph County, Michigan. As trustee, I participated in local governance through the agency of town meetings. At these events, held in the town hall at regular intervals, anyone could show up (and did), and anyone could spout off (and did) on any topic they wanted. I loved it. It was government at its most local and grassroots. Truthfully, it was probably government at its most effective, too. In any case, it was certainly government at its most engaged with the ordinary person, and in my later years as a congressman, I often participated in similar meetings.

Now, in the aftermath of 9/11, I needed to know what people were thinking and feeling, so we decided to hold our own town hall meetings. In the reigning climate of hostility and paranoia, holding these sessions in a literal town hall was not feasible. Instead, we called our meetings in private homes. The first was in a home in Philadelphia, where we met with a group of about thirty influential Muslim members of the community—doctors, lawyers, professors, imams, and others. For several hours, we listened to them talk about how frustrated they were, about how, in the City of Brotherly Love, they were being treated like criminals.

"We are patriotic Americans," one man said. "We love America. America has given us our chance. But we are being looked down upon, shunned and ostracized, made to feel guilty, as if we were complicit in these crimes simply because we are Muslims."

We shared some of our findings about the bridges we had discovered between the East and West, and they got very excited. Some of the people who hosted these meetings have since become close friends and are still in regular contact with us.

We held another meeting in New Jersey, at the home of a doctor named Mohammed Kawam. The Kawam family put out a spread of some of the best food I've ever tasted. The hospitality was overwhelmingly thoughtful and kind (a regular occurrence, I've noticed, in our many travels in Muslim countries). At this meeting, we heard pretty much the same things we'd heard in Philadelphia. Afterward, we sat down with Dr. Kawam to talk over the evening's experiences. He said, "Mark, you know, you are the only person who has done this."

"Done what?" I asked. "The only nonpolitician to hold a town meeting in your town?"

"No," he explained, "the only person to talk to us. Period. To really ask us what it's like for us, what's going on for us."

I felt a strange, momentary flutter of déjà vu. When had I had this conversation before? Later that evening, when I was alone and had some time to mull it over, it hit me. Of course. When I was at the United Nations, meeting with permanent representatives from forty-one countries around the world. *You are the only diplomat so far to ask me a single question that goes deeper than the weather or the state of Manhattan traffic.* We don't talk to other nations, and now we weren't talking to our own citizens.

Back on the Hill, people wondered why on earth I was doing this. "What are you doing, Mark? You're not running for office, are you?" But it had nothing to do with running for anything, or with politics at all. It was something I needed to do, both for them and for myself. They needed to have someone listen. And I needed to hear what they had to say.

These early town meetings were just the beginning. We continued to meet at least every month or every other month, and also began meeting with a series of influential people from both Muslim and Christian backgrounds, talking about what we were observing and sharing our experiences.

My network of Muslim friends continued to grow, and despite my initial financial worries after 9/11, we managed to step up our schedule of foreign travel—financed by my own earnings but also, more and more, by that growing network of friends, which now included both committed Christians and a growing number of committed Muslims.

A FEW YEARS later, Abdel and I traveled together to Africa, a trip that included visits to Cameroon, Nairobi, and his homeland, Sudan, where we met with President al-Bashir and many of his top advisors, along with many of the political and intellectual elite of the country. Everywhere we went, we spoke about bridges between our cultures and were met with great interest and amazingly open minds and hearts. But the level of responsiveness we found was not, I believe, prompted so much by what we said as by who we were: a white Christian American and a Sudanese Muslim imam traveling together, the best of friends. It blew their minds.

"We live today in a world full of suspicion and fear," one man told us, "but when we see the two of you talking and laughing and praying together, suddenly we are able to see a vision of West and East being friends."

Abdel grew very quiet.

"Listen," he said, "what you are saying is so true. Had Mark and I met twenty years ago, when I first came to America, I would not have crossed the street to spit on an infidel like him. And from what he has told me, I think it would have been much the same the other way around."

And of course he was right. When I wrote that angry letter of protest after hearing the Qur'an read at a Prayer Breakfast event, I was reacting just as my culture had taught me to react, just as Abdel would have reacted to me according to how his culture had taught him. Had we met at that time, we would have stood on two opposing riverbanks, separated by the boiling river of contempt and misunderstanding that has been running unchecked for centuries and today threatens to surge out of its riverbed and flood the earth.

But in those days immediately after 9/11, as we watched the world polarize and the gulf of suspicion divide communities and nations, it seemed more critical than ever to put old prejudices aside and seek first to understand—to reach out and talk, just as friends. In those days, hardly anyone from outside the Muslim communities was talking to them. And *nobody* was actually *listening* to them.

FOURTEEN

Jihad

Even as my friends and I were looking for ways to reach out across the Christian-Muslim divide, the world, it seemed, was rapidly growing more polarized than ever, making the task both more urgent and more difficult.

From the day the planes hit the towers, the conflict was cast in terms of world war. On September 12, less than twenty-four hours after the attacks, NATO invoked Article 5 of the North Atlantic Treaty and declared that the actions against the World Trade Center and the Pentagon were in fact hostilities taken against all nineteen membership countries of NATO. The White House immediately began talking about a "global war on terror." In an address to a joint session of Congress on September 20, President Bush declared that this war "will not end until every terrorist group of global reach has been found and defeated." By October 7, less than a month after the attacks in New York and Washington, D.C., we had invaded Afghanistan. In an address a few days later, the president said, "The world has come together to fight a new and different war."

But exactly what *was* this global war? "New" how? "Different" why?

To much of the Muslim East, as my growing circle of Muslim friends pointed out, this looked like a very old war indeed, and one initiated not by Muslim militants but by the West. On Sunday, September 16, President Bush told reporters, "This crusade, this war on terrorism, is going to take a while." His statement caused an uproar, and within days the White House was backpedaling and apologizing for the president's use of the word "crusade," insisting that he only meant to say that the global fight against terrorism was a "broad cause." Whether Freudian slip or innocent gaffe, the phrase struck a nerve throughout the Arab world. And no wonder. It only served to confirm their worst fears: that this global war emerging from the ashes of the fallen towers would be cast in the horrific but familiar terms of one religion's efforts to wipe out another.

And this was not hypersensitivity on the Muslim community's part. The very word "crusade" derives from the French word *croisade*, meaning "marked by the cross." Only in modern times has it come to have the meaning "broad cause." Historically it has meant not a "broad cause" but a very specific one: the righteous battle against evil—the holy war.

Ever since the days of Ayatollah Khomeini, when pictures of American presidents were routinely burned in effigy and the United States first found itself being lambasted as "the Great Satan," Americans have been genuinely perplexed by the hatred and vitriol displayed toward us by Islamic peoples of the East. From our vantage point, we are a noble, God-fearing nation, generous with our gifts to the poor and disaster-stricken of other countries. Americans give more aid, per capita, to the impoverished than do the citizens of any other country in the world. We are a country of freedom, apple pie, and soccer moms. Who would hate that?

But to the Muslim communities of the East, as I was now learning, this all smacks of a morally superior attitude buoyed by a blatant double standard. The United States condemns terror and its financing networks, yet the same thing occurs right in its own backyard. Many of the weapons Saddam used during his regime were provided, directly or indirectly, by the United States. Indeed, the Stinger missiles being used by Taliban forces against Americans were supplied by the Americans themselves, back in the days when we were supporting Afghanistan in its efforts to fend off the invading Soviet Union.

It has been said that "one man's Mede is another man's Persian"—or to put a finer point on it, one man's *terrorist* is another man's *freedom fighter*. The United States classifies Hezbollah (whose name means "the party of God") as a terrorist organization. But this perspective cuts both ways: according to Avi Jorisch, a specialist in Arab media who has worked for the Pentagon, "Hezbollah views *America* as a terrorist state."[1] And many Muslims view key Israeli figures, such as former prime minister Menachem Begin, as terrorists.

As the war of words heated to a boil in the days after 9/11, it seemed to me that arguments supporting or denying either point of view were missing the point, which was how widely and fiercely both perspectives were held. The West viewed Islam as being dedicated to the destruction of the West. The Islamic East saw the "war on terror" as a war against their religion and way of life. Noted Islamic scholar John Esposito summarized the dilemma this way:

> For the Christian West, Islam is the religion of the sword; for Muslims, the Christian West is epitomized by the armies of the Crusades.[2]

It was shaping up as an intractable standoff. The Muslim world saw the West as unrepentantly expansionist, a people who would stop at nothing until we had forced our own cultural, economic, political, and religious way of life on all the populations of the planet. To the Muslim East, Christianity was not a true faith but a faith that had been corrupted and hijacked to serve our imperialistic ways.

I sat over lunch one day with Girma Asmerom, then the Eritrean ambassador to the United States, and listened as he confessed his deep-seated feelings about European colonialism. "The white man brought us Christianity, the Bible, and prayer," Girma told me. "He told us to read the Bible and look up and pray. We did. When we were finished praying and looked down again, our land was gone." This was the view from the eastern side of the divide.

And the view from the West seemed scarcely any different. To the average citizen of the Judeo-Christian West, especially in these post-9/11 days, Islam seemed to have one underlying agenda: to conquer and utterly vanquish the West.

These two viewpoints, how the Islamic East sees the Christian West and vice versa, continue to prevail today, and of course, neither view is any more accurate than the other. Unfortunately, though, a handful of demagogues and radical clerics have hijacked the genuine faith of Islam and engaged us in a war of ideology, amplified by hateful Western condemnation of Islam, the Qur'an, and the prophet Muhammad—and the escalating rhetoric on both sides of the battle threatens to turn their worst scenarios into self-fulfilling prophecies. There is perhaps no better example of this deliberate, emotionally supercharged distorting of crucial terms and concepts than the case of the word "jihad."

Jihad: in the post-9/11 world, few terms evoke a more visceral reaction, on both sides of the East-West divide. The idea of jihad is held up as a banner, rallying the cause of Muslim radicals. Ask anyone on the street, East or West, "What is jihad?" and chances are excellent the answer you'll get will be some variation of this: "Jihad is the 'holy war' of Islam against infidels, that is, all non-Muslims." But is that true? What does the word actually mean?

In the waning days of 2001, as the days grew shorter and the rhetoric on all sides grew hotter, it seemed critical to gain a complete understanding of this term "jihad" for myself, so I sat down to go through the entire Qur'an, page by page, and examine every single *aya* that deals with this concept. What I learned was fascinating.

"Jihad" is used in the Qur'an primarily to describe the *struggle* or *striving* against negative influences in the pursuit of internal purity. It is also commonly used in defensive terms: struggling against sin and vanity, avoiding contacts with unbelievers and other corrupting influences, much like the "shunning" practiced by the Amish in America.

The term has many shades of meaning. In different suras of the Qur'an, "jihad" is used variously to denote: avoiding unbelievers and hypocrites, striving to convince and encourage, having faith, dealing with money and self, emigration, patience, and giving. "Jihad" covers the one who struggles in the righteous path of internal purification, the reward that awaits those who righteously struggle thus, and righteousness itself.

Some passages in the Qur'an use "jihad" to describe defensive fighting in the cause of Allah, which is readily taken out of context to imply armed aggression; but this is poles apart from the genuine Qur'anic meaning. The struggle to defend family, friends, community, and honor against external attack is also jihad, but this use of the term appears as such in the Qur'an only rarely—certainly far less often (and with far less vivid evocations of bloodshed) than the same impulse is described in the Old Testament.

What the term means primarily is an *internal struggle,* the effort to withstand external influences and come closer to God. When James, the brother of Jesus, invokes the word "religion," he defines it as giving to orphans and widows, plus the effort to *keep oneself pure in the world.* This struggle to keep oneself pure, untainted, and clear in mind, body, and soul, is jihad.

Interestingly, the Peshitta version of the New Testament uses an eerily similar word in Aramaic, *geeakh*—pronounced *ji'ah*—

which likewise means "to strive" (e.g., Matt. 12:19, Col. 1:29, Heb. 12:4). Both the Qur'an and New Testament use the term "jihad" as a struggle or fight, not against external forces or enemies but for *internal* peace and to get closer to God. It is exactly this struggle that Paul describes so eloquently in his great letter to the believers in Rome:

> For it is not the good that I wish to do, that I do: but it is the evil that I do not wish to do, that I do. (Rom. 7:19)

This same sense of jihad is apparent when Jesus finds himself alone in the garden of Gethsemane, knowing of his betrayal and impending capture, and struggling with himself to accept his fate. From Jesus to Paul to Augustine to Luther, all the great figures of Christianity have described their own vivid experience with that same jihad described so beautifully in the florid classical Arabic of the Qur'an.

As intriguing as it was to begin understanding the full scope, majesty, and especially cultural commonality of the term, it didn't take long to realize where the essential problem lay: too many Muslims today don't really know what the Qur'an says.

If someone told you that the Bible laid out a blueprint for the pogroms of Europe that burned thousands of Jews at the stake, or for the Inquisition in Spain that expelled hundreds of thousands of Jews and forced conversions under torture, you might fiercely object—and of course, you'd be right to do so. But during those horrendous times, very few people actually *read* the Bible (in *any* language, let alone the Semitic languages that best convey its original meaning), because the majority of the population was illiterate. When their leaders told them that in the name of God they were supposed to go torture and rape and murder people, that's what they did.

This is not all that different from the situation today. Just as a lot of Westerners know the Bible only vaguely (and consider themselves "Christians" because their parents were, or because they occasionally go to church), quite a few Muslims really don't know the Qur'an well at all. Muslim clerics say that the Qur'an can be fully understood only in its original Arabic. Yet of the 1.2 billion Muslims worldwide, barely 15 percent can read Arabic, and a great many of that 15 percent would find the ornate language of classical, seventh-century Arabic daunting. (Imagine how many modern Americans or Britons would be able to read *Beowulf* in its original Anglo-Saxon, and you get an idea of the scope of the problem.)

The plain truth is that few Muslims in today's world are genuinely conversant with the actual text of the Qur'an. Just like the Europeans of those earlier centuries, modern Muslims rely on their religious and political leadership to tell them what it says. (In the same way, I would guess that far fewer than 1 percent of modern Christians can actually read the Aramaic or Greek New Testament, and therefore they also rely on the interpretations of translations and religious leaders.) In great part, the problem of Muslim terrorism is one of ignorance of their own holy book and the core tenets of faith. Islam has been "dumbed down" to serve the goals of radical militancy. Militants, when unable to justify their deviant interpretations with the Qur'an, also manipulate jihad through the lenses of Islam's other important (though not inspired) books, the Hadith and Sunnah.

The Qur'an tells us that Muhammad was compassionate even in war: he prohibited the killing or ill treatment of women and children and even forbade the cutting down of trees. The image of impressionable, fanatical young men and women striding into public places with explosives strapped to their chests to blow apart scores of a randomly executed public—or of jumbo jets filled with innocent civilians hijacked and flown into buildings filled with thousands more—would have filled the prophet of Mecca and Medina with revulsion and horror.

This is the awful irony of it: just as Adolf Hitler hijacked the concept of personal purity before God, or "Christian purity," and distorted it into the justification for a campaign of genocide, the promoters of Muslim militancy have hijacked what is in essence the same principle—the personal struggle to reach and maintain inner purity—and harnessed it to a campaign of mass murder.

In their blood-strewn agendas of militant aggression, the Crusaders, the Inquisitors, the Nazis, and the so-called Jihadists all claim moral superiority and a mandate direct from on high. And it is all a lie: none of it has anything to do with God or Allah, nor with Jesus or Muhammad or "purity" or "jihad." It is wholly the invention of the bitter heart of human hatred—and it's time we exposed the lie for what it is, instead of simply throwing screamed insults, threats, and bombs at it.

The more I learned about this concept, its background and true meaning, the more I realized that we in the West were unwittingly encouraging, through our use of such phrases as "the ideology of terror" and similar characterizations of the "Islamic terrorist agenda," the very distortions that lay at the heart of the problem. If these vulnerable Muslim men and women were being told by radical militants that jihad was a "holy war" against the infidels of the West (especially Christian and Jews) based on the Holy Qur'an, and they then heard a consistent chorus of confirmation from the West, telling them that indeed, the Qur'an promotes violence—weren't we simply affirming the fanatics' distortion of their own holy book?

Our strategy for addressing Muslim militancy should be based not on confirming their *tafsir* (interpretation) of the Qur'an but on *challenging* it: present a peaceful point of view and let the truth prevail. This has to be the first step toward mitigating terrorism.

OF COURSE, THERE is more to Muslim terrorism than a manipulated mantra. There are many facets to the cultural rift between East and West that are invoked to inflame anti-Western sentiment and the perceived need to defend against Western aggression, and these all help to feed the fires of Holy War. But there is one driving force, beyond all the others, behind the extremists' most fearsome and unstoppable weapon. That weapon is the suicide attacker, the martyr-soldier, and the driving force behind it is that powerful and time-tested motivation for militancy: the promise of salvation.

Every single sura in the Qur'an but one (the ninth) begins with these words: *Bismi' Llah al-Rahman al-Rahim*, "In the name of Allah the benevolent and merciful. . . ."[3] However, although Allah is merciful, there is a common belief in Islam that one cannot know for sure whether that forgiveness will be applied to oneself, individually, until Judgment Day. This determination may be influenced, for example, by how faithful one has been to the five pillars of Islam.

Actually, there are Qur'anic passages that are quite clear on the surety of salvation. For example, sura 3:31 says, "Allah will love you and forgive you your sins." And look at the majestically redemptive message in this passage:

> Those who believe [in the Qur'an] and those who follow the Jewish [scriptures] and the Christians and the Sabians [Aramaic-speaking sects of Christians]—any who believe in Allah and the Last Day, and work righteousness, shall have their reward with their Lord; on them shall be no fear, nor shall they grieve. (sura 2:62)

However, on this topic as on most, the Qur'an tends to be somewhat delphic and open to interpretation. As Catholic University professor Sidney Griffith, one of the world's leading experts on Semitic languages, describes it, "The Qur'an is rarely a direct declaration; it is allusive. It assumes its audience already knows the stories and context from which it speaks."[4]

The architects of militant Muslim ideology have homed in on the "uncertainty of salvation" concept and provided a black and white answer: there is only one way to guarantee that Allah's benevolent mercy will be applied in one's individual case, and that is martyrdom—specifically, to give up one's life in the act of destroying infidels. This, they say, is jihad: the holy war, the righteous cause, the one sure path to eternal bliss.

Which, of course, is pure nonsense. The Qur'an doesn't prescribe murder or suicide as a path to salvation any more than the Bible does. But that didn't stop Pope Urban II from claiming that anyone who took up arms to participate in the church's war against the East (in what history would later call the First Crusade) would automatically earn full penance. And it hasn't stopped Muslim extremists from successfully promoting the idea of jihad as its own brand of religiously sanctioned, holy-cause-justified, God-endorsed rationale for mass murder.

As SOME FRIENDS and I sat over dinner in Bahrain with a group of Muslim political, business, and religious leaders, I was struck with a thought about this terrible cycle of doctrine-inspired fanaticism: much of the rationale of Muslim militancy and martyrdom rests on the nobility of defending Islam from infidels, which includes killing them. But if their definition of "infidels" is simply "all those who are not Muslims," I thought, what happens when we take a closer look at the definition of what it means to be a Muslim? After waiting for an appropriate lull in the conversation, I posed this question to the group: "Let's imagine we had a Jew, a Christian, and a Muslim sitting together around a table much like this one, talking about their traditions and their different holy scriptures. And then let's imagine that the Muslim is explaining what it means to be a Muslim, telling the other two about the Muslim witness of faith, the Shahada, and the Jew suddenly exclaims, 'Wait! In our own holy book it says almost exactly the same thing!'"

The men stopped me, vigorously shaking their heads and saying, "No, no, not possible."

I said, "I can prove it to you."

One of them said, "Well, you're going to have to, because as far as I can see, this is impossible."

I said, "Would you agree that Moses and Jesus were both Jews?" He nodded, and I continued. "The Qur'an says that they were both Muslims, so somewhere within their practice of Judaism, mustn't they have said the Shahada?" The men were silent. "In Deuteronomy it says—may I speak Hebrew?"

"Of course," they said.

I went on to explain the meaning of Shema ("The Lord our God, the Lord is one"), that it is virtually identical to Shahada ("There is no God but Allah"), and that they both say essentially the same thing. And that when asked what was the greatest commandment of all, Jesus (as recorded in Mark's Gospel) repeated the Shema, and went on to define the state of complete surrender to God—in heart, mind, soul, and action—that is the essence of the word "Muslim."

"Back to our circle of friends," I said. "If they all discover they are saying essentially the same Shahada, and embracing the same state of being in submission to God, the same *shalem*, what would that make them?"

They were silent at first, and then began whispering to each other in Arabic. Finally one man, a highly esteemed Sudanese *sheikh*, spoke up. "They would be, in essence, *Muslims.*"

"Now I'm not saying that they would be Muslims in every sense," I hastened to add, "certainly not culturally, and not in every aspect of their practice. They would retain their own cultural values, religions, and traditions. But at the very least, one couldn't really consider any of them *infidels*, could one?"

"No," came his stunned reply. "One couldn't."

•   •   •

As stunned as my *sheikh* friend was at this thought, I was even more excited at its implications. What happens to the martyr's cause, I reasoned, if we suddenly have no clear definition of "infidel"? If one man's infidel turns out to be another man's Muslim? If there is no one to kill, no one to blow up with our suicide bombs, no one for us to use as targets while we martyr ourselves gloriously in our righteous cause?

The driving force behind the terrifying power of Muslim extremism is also its Achilles' heel. Because if we can demonstrate a critical flaw in this idea, the whole strategy begins to unravel. And what could be a more fatal flaw in the logic of the Muslim suicide bomber than the idea that a Jew or Christian might be, as this group of esteemed Muslim holy men in Bahrain confirmed, "in essence, a Muslim"?

My American imam friend told me he describes such a person as a "spiritual Muslim."

"It's not about comparing or contrasting anything," he said. "Being a *spiritual Muslim* is a state of being—in body, mind, and soul—where an individual totally and unconditionally surrenders himself to God as his only master and creator. It is that special feeling of indebtedness for his very existence that develops in a spiritual Muslim an inner sense of humility toward God and the universe."

One who enters into this state of being, said Abdel, becomes a humble human being, working to benefit others simply because he or she was created equal by the same One God. Thus a genuine sense of love, brotherhood, and peace naturally develops for every other individual fellow human without exception.

Indeed, this process could be the spark of hope to curtail the East's view of a modern Crusade by a militaristic, expansionist West and the West's view of a mysterious, distant religion bent on their destruction.

It seemed to me that this common ground of better understanding held the power to dispel Western ignorance and dis-
mantle the entire machinery of Muslim extremism with its
armies of willing suicide bombers. When we accept this idea of a
"spiritual Muslim," it's easy to see that anyone of faith—whether
in the Jewish or Christian tradition or, for that matter, in any
other tradition—can enter into this same state of being and
become submitted to God: a fellow seeker pursuing his own
jihad on the path to *shalem*.

FIFTEEN

Scrutiny

I looked out at my audience: 150 Christian missionaries and doctors of theology gathered for a conference in Gatlinburg, Tennessee, all waiting to hear what I had to say about Islam. It was no mystery what they were *expecting* me to say: Islam is of the devil, a pernicious corruption of faith that is bent on the destruction of everything we believe in. I wondered how they would react to the message I had actually come to bring them.

"Do you mind," I began, "if I open with some passages from scripture?"

Assuming I was referring to the Bible, they said, "Please do!"

"Jesus is the Messiah," I intoned, "sinless, supernaturally conceived through a virgin named Mary by the spirit of God, was taken up to be close to God and will be the judge of the world.... He is the Word of God, He is the Word of Truth.... He heals the sick and the blind, He can even raise the dead."

Everyone in the audience was listening in rapt attention, nodding their heads, some calling out "Hallelujah!" and "Praise the Lord!" Then I stopped and looked up at them.

"Every word I just spoke came from the Qur'an."

Their animated gesticulations froze in mid-gesture. The place fell silent, so deathly quiet I could actually hear the sound of my own heart beating. And then someone in the back proclaimed in an audible whisper, *"Liar!"*

Anticipating a challenge, I'd brought my copy of the Qur'an with me. I pulled it out and proceeded to show them, line for line, sura for sura, where every single word I'd said was written. The moderator of the event had to call a halt in the day's schedule. The seminarians lined up for hours to talk with me, one by one, not because they were angry but because they were shocked and fascinated. They could hardly believe what they were hearing, yet they knew this was no hoax or academic sleight of hand. They knew my reputation and Christian background, and most of all, they saw the evidence of their eyes: there was the text, just as I'd said. It was irrefutable. They were dumbfounded.

THIS SCENE TOOK place in the spring of 2000, long before the events of 9/11. In the end, the members of this group offered no serious challenges to my conclusions. But what about now, I wondered a few years later, thinking back to that day from the perspective of the post-9/11 world. Would we still find the same receptivity and fascination if we played that scene over again today? And even if we did, speaking for a few hours to a conference in Gatlinburg, Tennessee, was one thing. What would the world's top experts in linguistics and religion have to say about these ideas?

As my Muslim friends and I continued to cross-reference our cultures and religious traditions, exploring in depth every avenue of common ground we could find, I began compiling our findings into a research document. As the document grew lengthier and lengthier, we realized that we needed to take a crucial next step before we could think about releasing these findings to the world at large.

We felt sure we were onto something of critical importance to the world. But were we simply being naïve, victims of our own wishful thinking? Would our findings stand up to the highest level of academic and theological scrutiny? The only way we could know for sure was to begin sharing this growing document with top academic and religious leaders all over the world.

The opportunity came soon enough, when I was invited by a friend to give a lecture over the phone to his students in Edinburgh, Scotland. This friend was director of the Center for Muslim-Christian studies, which is affiliated with the University of Edinburgh. I readily agreed, and this soon turned into a full-blown invitation for a two-day lecture series at the University of Edinburgh.

It was only when we arrived on the campus in Edinburgh that it began to dawn on me just how intimidating this whole thing was. My presentation was to be facilitated by Dr. Yasir Suleiman, a Palestinian Muslim scholar and the author of several authoritative books on the Arabic language, who also serves as head of the Edinburgh Institute for the Study of the Arab World and Islam. I was to present my lectures in the Playfair Library at the University of Edinburgh, where Arabic had been taught for some 240 years. The place was filled with busts and gilt-edged photographs and portraits of many generations of professors. For some reason, I had thought I would be speaking to a handful of professors in a cozy conference room. Not so. We were ushered into the lecture hall early to take a preliminary look at the surroundings. There were over a hundred finely burnished hardwood chairs lined up with mathematical precision. To say I felt out of my league would be putting it mildly.

Before leaving the States, I had told my friend Cal Thomas, the nationally syndicated columnist, what we were doing. Cal, who is known for his blunt delivery and stadium voice, wasted no time in telling me what he thought about that: "Are you kidding? You're gonna get eaten *aliiive*! They're *Europeans*, you know—Europeans *hate* Americans, and they hate politicians even *more*! And to make it even worse, you're going in there to tell them that you found something they, the experts, all missed for the last fourteen hundred years? They're going to think you're arrogant and *eat you aliiiive!*"

Standing there in the prestigious Playfair Library, the finest building of its kind in all of Scotland, I realized that my friend was absolutely correct. This was, as we government employees used to say, way above my pay grade.

Within a few minutes the place was packed, row upon row of straight-backed chairs filled with straight-backed Brits, Scots, and others, every one of them scowling and looking very much like they were, in fact, going to *eat me aliiive*. Nancy leaned in close and whispered, "Oh, Mark, I'm going to be praying for you," and then took her seat in the audience.

We'd had a reception before the lecture where we had been introduced to Yasir Suleiman, and I startled him by speaking to him in Arabic. He was shocked. Their view is that most Americans can barely speak English (at least the way it's supposed to be spoken), let alone any other language. We had connected immediately, and that connection now paid off: his introduction was one of the kindest and most gracious I'd ever had. That was the good news. The bad news was, after it was over, it was my turn to speak.

Well, why don't I start off with a little joke, I thought. I glanced up at the ornately carved ceiling trim, the gilt-framed paintings everywhere, the most elegant, stately setting one could imagine, took a breath, and made my joke.

I don't even remember what it was. All I remember is that the punch line was greeted with thunderous silence. Among my austere, esteemed, learned audience members, I could not detect the slightest change in expression.

Lord, this isn't going well, I thought. *I'm about to be totally humiliated.* And then I felt a sense of lightening, as if a refreshing breeze had wafted through the room. *You don't need to impress them, Mark. You just need to tell the truth.* I closed my carefully crafted notes and looked up at the waiting faces lining the ancient room. *You don't need to be some dumb American politician telling them they missed something. Just be yourself.* I cleared my throat and started over.

"I've discovered some ... some rather surprising things," I began, "and over the past few years, my colleagues and I have embarked on a journey that has taken us into areas that I had never imagined existed. That is to say, I've been compiling a list of similarities between the Aramaic New Testament and the Arabic Qur'an, along with some overlay of the Hebrew Tanach, looking for overlaps, correspondences, and convergences."

They were listening, that much was clear, but with what inflection or attitude it was impossible to say. Still, at least they weren't stopping me or arguing—yet—so I continued.

"We know there are over three hundred words with Aramaic roots used in the original text of the Qur'an. There's been a good deal written about these and about the sprinkling of Aramaic words found in the Greek New Testament, as you know. But those writings are quite limited in their scope. What we're looking for here is textual synergies that can have a practical impact in the world of our culture and society at large, not only in academic circles, and even help in our efforts to mitigate the gaping chasm of fear and misunderstanding between the cultures of the Muslim East and Judeo-Christian West.

"I have no formal background in linguistics, comparative religion, or Islamic studies. My academic background is in political science and history, and it is from these perspectives that I first undertook this course of study. I approach these fascinating issues as an amateur—an *amateur* in the true sense of the word, of *one who pursues his subject out of love,* out of a personal passion for the matter at hand. I've come here today because I hope to get your input on these ideas, to see what you think about it all."

At this last point, their body language finally began to change. Yasir broke into a smile. He chimed in and told his assembled colleagues that he hoped they would indeed take me up on this point and offer me their views on what we discussed. All at once the atmosphere shifted and became distinctly collegial. Out of the corner of my eye, I saw Nancy let out a sigh of relief.

The lecture actually turned out rather well. In fact, I gave two more lectures over the following days. About a month later I got a call telling me that the audio CD of the lecture had circulated around their community. Not everyone at Edinburgh had agreed with my ideas in their entirety, but there was warm appreciation for my personal manner of negotiation using Jesus as common ground, and the use of Aramaic as a bridge to Arabic-speaking Muslims stimulated keen interest.

NOT LONG AFTER my Edinburgh experience, I received an invitation from the award-winning novelist T. Davis Bunn (*The Quilt*, *The Great Divide*, and others) to come to England to give a talk in the most prestigious academic setting I could imagine: Regent's Park College at Oxford University. Bunn and I did not know each other (I had been recommended by a mutual friend), and it was clear that the invitation came with a sense of caution attached. He e-mailed me to ask what I would be speaking on, adding, "We've had Muslims, Jews, and Christians all come and speak. The Muslims and Jews have been substantive, but the Christians always embarrass me with their bombastic speeches and shallow, broad generalities."

I wrote back and said not to worry, I promised it would be fine. He replied and asked if it would be possible to send over my talk in writing ahead of time. "No," I answered, "but I'll bring it with me when I come," and again, I reassured him that my talk would not be an embarrassment.

Not only was it not an embarrassment—in fact, Davis was so excited about the talk that we have collaborated ever since: he is now an advisor and is helping us work on the idea of an English-language television program for the Al Jazeera network on finding bridges between Muslim and Christian cultures.

THE EDINBURGH AND Oxford experiences proved not to be unique. Over the following years I've had the opportunity to share these thoughts at length with a wide range of top academics in pertinent fields, nearly always with the same positive results.

For example, I brought our ideas to Joseph Cumming, director of the Reconciliation Program of the Center for Faith and Culture at Yale Divinity School. Cumming is perhaps best known as a Christian Arab linguist. Born and raised in New York, he has spent most of his adult life in the Islamic Republic of Mauritania (a neighbor of the Western Sahara, where my adventures in exploring these bridges between cultures began) and speaks Arabic better than most Arabs. He and I have spent many hours together going over many of these ideas in great detail.

Over the past few years, I've also been privileged to spend several sessions speaking with Dr. Father Sidney Griffith of the Semitics Department at Catholic University in Washington, D.C., who is a prominent scholar on the Semitic languages. Still, Joseph Cumming, Dr. Griffith, and the other academics and authors we've had the opportunity to speak with, while experts with impeccable credentials and professional objectivity, all hail from a decidedly Western, Christian perspective. I soon began wondering, what about top-flight academics from other cultures, from Jewish and Muslim backgrounds? Fortunately, our travels in Africa and the Mideast provided ready access to such authorities.

In the past few years we have been able to spend a good deal of time in Jerusalem with quite a few academic experts, including Dr. Eldon Clem, a top Syriac (Aramaic) scholar in Israel. Eldon is a Messianic Jew[1] who speaks fluently several different dialects of Syriac Aramaic and Hebrew, and two of Greek. I can't think of anyone in the world more fluidly at home in the textual worlds we were seeking to bridge: a Jew who embraced Jesus and was a world-class expert in Aramaic. Eldon went over our thick research document and commented that it was some of the most important work he'd ever read.

We visited the American University in Beirut and talked with professors and students there, then continued on to Amman, the capital city of Jordan, to talk with two of the top advisors to King Abdullah II bin al-Hussein—a man whose mission is to build a moderate Islamic force in the Mideast.

From there we went to Ramallah, a Palestinian city about six miles north of Jerusalem in the West Bank. The most cosmopolitan of the cities in the Palestinian territories, Ramallah housed Arafat in his final years and is where he was buried. The place has an extraordinary history. In 1993, on the day Arafat shook hands with Yitzhak Rabin at the White House, Palestinian children in Ramallah were photographed handing olive branches to the Israeli soldiers who patrolled their streets. Alas, the city has been far less peaceful in recent years.

In Ramallah we were able to speak to several small gatherings of Arab scholars. In view of the city's unique place in modern Muslim history, I was especially touched when they responded to our findings and ideas every bit as enthusiastically as had the scholars at Edinburgh, Oxford, Yale, and Catholic University.

In another trip, I lectured at a peace event in Cairo sponsored by the U.S. Federation for Middle East Peace, a U.N.-approved NGO based in New York and run by two Lebanese Muslims. Once again, our audience was a group of largely Muslim listeners, and once again, they were as receptive and positive a group as any we'd encountered.

After hearing about these findings and perspectives, top advisors such as Dr. Ali Treky (the Qaddafi advisor I'd befriended in the States) and Dr. Ahmed Abbadi (Islamic advisor to the king of Morocco) invited us to come talk with their bosses. (Such invitations do not come lightly; there are reputations and high positions on the line.) Indeed, everywhere we traveled, in the Middle East, North Africa, and South Asia, we encountered Muslim religious scholars, academicians, businessmen, politicians, and media figures by the dozens who, while not necessarily agreeing 100 percent with everything we said, found the ideas captivating and groundbreaking. Many spoke about these ideas' potential "to change the world" (in their words).

Still, as positive as the professors and researchers were, I felt we had not yet met our toughest potential critics. Since that first trip to the Sahrawi refugee camp on the edge of Algeria, we had befriended many Muslim leaders. But what would the most arch-conservative Christian religious leaders have to say? Once again, we would not have to wait long for an answer.

ONE DAY AS I was having lunch with my friend and advisor Bill Aramony at a restaurant in Arlington, I heard a voice I recognized. I looked around, and my eye fell on John Nakamura, an old friend and colleague of Tony Hall's. When President Bush appointed Tony as the U.S. ambassador to the U.N. Food Program in Rome, John went to Rome with him. They met some of the top people in Rome, some of the pope's friends, and one of them joined John's prayer group.

John had returned from Rome, bringing with him this gentleman, Mario, whom I took to be Italian, and they happened to be dining at the same restaurant as we were. We went through our introductions, and John said, "Mark, would you share with our friend from Rome what you're doing with the Muslims?"

It turned out that Mario was not Italian after all but came from Malta, where a form of Arabic is spoken, so when I began explaining the Arabic words, he immediately knew what I was talking about.

"This could be revolutionary!" he said. I suppressed a smile. This seems to be the word that invariably springs to people's lips when they first encounter the idea of the underlying unity of Islam, Christianity, and Judaism, and it has become so predictable that it makes me smile (at least inwardly) every time. "But," he continued, "are you sure this is all correct?" I said that as best as we'd been able to find, it was. He said, "You need to come speak to some of the scholars in Rome about this."

"You set it up," said Bill, "and we'll come."

So he did—and we did. He arranged a meeting with a professor of comparative religion and a priest who is head of the Religion Department at one of the pontifical universities. Bill and I flew to Rome and took a car to Vatican City, which is not only the seat of authority over the world's 1.2 billion Catholics but also enjoys the distinction of being the smallest independent nation on the planet.

We found our way to the meeting and proceeded to spend a good two and a half hours with our hosts, captivated by our magnificent and historic surroundings. They were very gracious, very serious, and very excited. "This is absolutely—" and I knew the word that was coming, "revolutionary!"

"You think so?" I said.

"Absolutely! I've never heard of anything like this before."

"Really?" This was not a rhetorical question. It genuinely surprised me that a professor of comparative religion and a priest at the Vatican would have never heard anything quite like what we were proposing.

"Absolutely," the professor repeated. "And in fact, I would like to invite you to write a paper for our pontifical publication."[2] After our talk, the priest also invited us to visit the interior of the Vatican vault to read some Aramaic documents in the original—which, we were told, very few Catholics, let alone non-Catholics, are ever invited to do. Unfortunately, we were tightly scheduled and on our way to the Mideast, so we couldn't take them up on this extraordinary invitation. But it didn't really matter. To us, what mattered was their excitement and genuine enthusiasm.

OF THE MORE than two billion Christians in the world, about half are Catholics and some 27 percent are Protestants. Among Protestants, the most vocal and politically active, and certainly the most active in their denunciation of Islam, are the Evangelicals, that group of which I had once proudly counted myself a member. (These days, I try not to put myself into any boxes or act as a "member" of any club, and refer to myself simply as "a follower of Jesus.") We had now met with the highest academic authorities possible in the Catholic world, short of sitting down with a cardinal or the pope. The next question was, how would the Evangelical world greet our ideas?[3]

As if by clockwork, I soon received another call from Cal Thomas, who began the conversation, as is his style, by getting right to the point.

"Mark, I read your research document, and now I want to take you to see Ergun Caner." No "Hi, Mark," no "How are you?" I was used to it.

"Um, who's that?" I replied.

"Was a Turkish Muslim, came to America to convert us all to Islam. Got converted himself. Now he's head of Liberty Divinity School for Jerry Falwell."

I nearly gasped. "I don't—no, wait, I'm not sure that's such a good idea . . ."

"Nope, we've gotta go talk to him."

I thought this man would be the *worst* person to talk to, that he'd think I'd become a traitor to the cause—that he'd be diametrically against everything I had to say! But then I realized what I was thinking and stopped. What if that were true? If there really was such a strong possibility that he'd be in complete disagreement with our findings, well, wasn't that exactly what we needed to find out?

"Okay," I replied with no small measure of trepidation. "When will he be in Washington?"

"He doesn't come to Washington. We're going to him. I'm driving," was Cal's reply.

"You're kidding! You're going to drive me all the way to Lynchburg—over four hours away—just to meet with Jerry Falwell's Divinity School man?"

"Nope," he said, "Charlottesville. Only two hours. We're meeting halfway. It's all set up. Got reservations at a good restaurant. I'm treating."

A few days later, Cal picked me up and we headed out Route 66 to Route 29 south, bound for Charlottesville, home of Thomas Jefferson's Monticello and the halfway point between me and Jerry Falwell. Cal had heard me talk a little about the idea of bridging the East-West divide, but only a smattering, so for the entire two hours in the car he peppered me with questions. What about the Muslims, don't they all want to kill us? What about jihad, didn't Muhammad tell his followers to kill all the infidels? What about everyone who insists that Allah and the God of the Bible are completely different? By the time we approached the campus of the University of Virginia and circled in on our restaurant reservation, I felt as if I'd been shot at for two hours. I staggered out of the car and wondered how meeting Ergun Caner could be any worse.

In fact, it was remarkable. Caner, who is extremely intelligent and personable, also plied me with questions throughout our lunch, but this time I did not feel machine-gunned at all. It felt rather like an engaging and profoundly attentive debriefing.

At the end of our lunch, Caner nodded and said, "Well, doable, definitely doable. Mark, I agree with everything you've said. I can't say whether or not Jerry will agree. We'll see. But from what I've heard here in this last ninety minutes, I would wholeheartedly endorse everything you're suggesting."

In 2006, when I would travel again to Sudan to meet with President al-Bashir to talk about the crisis in Darfur, Dr. Caner would accompany me to witness the process firsthand. In fact, the sight of Dr. Caner, a Turkish Muslim turned Evangelical Christian, holding hands with the Muslim president of Sudan and leading him in prayer, has become one of the most evocative images I've ever beheld.

Cal and I got back in his car and headed north. For a few minutes, atypically, Cal was silent. Finally he spoke up. "Well, it's one of two things." I waited for him to continue. "One, you're completely insane."

He stopped again, and this time I knew he was waiting for my prompt, so I obediently asked, "And number two?"

"Number two," he replied, "you've actually got something here."

The encouragement and comments from the Vatican, from Ergun Caner, from world-famous academics and theologians, were impressive, exciting, and gratifying. But nothing could have been more encouraging than hearing this from my friend Cal.

SIXTEEN

On the Green Line Again

In February 2005 I was invited to a Middle East retreat, held as part of the annual National Prayer Breakfast, to speak to the group about Islam and Jesus. For the talks, I chose two topics: "Could Jesus Be the Son of God in Islam?" and "Can Christians Embrace the Five Pillars of Islam?" Three people who heard my talks that day came to me afterward with some extraordinary requests.

The first was the chief Islamic advisor to Muhammad Bin al-Hassan, the king of Morocco. This man, who presides over thirty thousand mosques in Morocco, was so excited about what he heard that he invited me to come to Rabat to talk directly with the king about it.

In my study at home there hangs a photo taken in the 1980s of me standing at a photo op in Morocco, meeting the previous king, Hassan II, who was the present king's father. I had visited him, toured his palace, and been treated to the kind of gracious yet somewhat vacuous hospitality that typifies the diplomatic experience. That's what we did as congressmen: toured palaces and said, "How wonderful it is to be here." Did we accomplish anything? A little good PR, perhaps, but otherwise, not much.

What a contrast, I thought. Now, twenty years later, with no official title, office, or authority, I had an invitation from the new king's advisor on Islamic affairs to come talk with the king, not about his palace or décor, but about something of genuine substance, even of potentially vast influence and reach: how we can build bridges between our cultures and help create a nonviolent revolution of the human heart.

The other two people who came to meet me after my talks were a Lebanese woman named Gina, who was a highly placed advisor to Lebanon's President Lahoud, and her husband Fouad, a widely regarded professor at the American University of Beirut. They told me they were intrigued with what I'd said in my presentations.

I was impressed with their gracious manner and keen intelligence, and thanked them. Their request, however, did not come up in this conversation. It was around an issue that did not surface until nearly a year later, near the end of 2005, when I received a phone call one day from Fouad.

"Mark," he said, "Gina and I are in Washington for a few days, and we'd like to see you." We made a date to get together, and soon the young couple was sitting across from me in my living room, their young daughter asleep on a couch behind me. Gina was quite pregnant: child number two was on her way.

Fouad spoke first. "Look," he said, clearly feeling a little awkward and not knowing just where to begin. "I am a Muslim. My wife is a Christian. We have this beautiful child, as you see, and Gina is now pregnant with our second. So . . ."

He glanced at Gina, but she showed no inclination to speak. This was clearly his time to talk, and whatever had to be said, he would have to say it.

"So, we've been having a discussion about how to bring up our children. Really, more a debate than a discussion. Actually, a very stressful debate."

I was pretty sure of what was coming next, and could not help but imagine how stressful these "debates" must have been, and how difficult it was for him to bring this to someone who was not far removed from being a complete stranger.

"She wants to tell our children about Jesus as the son of God," Fouad continued. "As divine. About the Crucifixion and all of that—and I don't want this. I want to prohibit her from doing this, because these ideas are totally contrary to my beliefs."

The woman under discussion simply sat, looking directly at me, neither glancing in her husband's direction nor saying a word.

He went on. "In your talk, I remember, you spoke about the idea of Jesus as the son of God. I don't remember exactly what you said, but somehow, at the time . . . well, at the time it seemed . . . reasonable. Can you explain that once more, here, for just the two of us?"

I knew we were on delicate ground. I took a few minutes to go through the whole matter of the word "begotten," and how neither the Greek nor the English correctly conveyed the female-stemmed Aramaic words that implied birth from a woman, not procreation from a man. That when you examined the actual language, what our scriptures actually said was that Jesus was the son of *Mary*—only conceived by the *kun faya kun* command of God, much as the elements of the universe had been called into being at the beginning of Creation.

When I'd finished, I stopped.

Fouad slowly nodded his head and said, "That's . . . that's amazing." He turned to his wife and said, "Okay. You can teach Isa as the son of God." Then he turned back to me and said, "Now, can you tell us again, what was it you were saying before, about the so-called deity of Jesus?"

I nodded and carefully took the two of them through an explanation of that issue as well. By the time I had related my experience of hearing two dozen Bengali scholars in Dhaka intoning, "Isa! Ahh . . . *Ruhallah! Ruhallah!*" no more than five minutes had passed. Fouad nodded his assent, turned to his wife, and said, "Okay, you can say the spirit in Isa was deified, no problem." Then he turned back to me once more, leaned closer with a look of great intensity, and said, "Now, tell me about the Crucifixion."

He had saved the most sensitive issue for last. As is the case for many Muslims, this was the issue in Christianity that seemed most abhorrent and irreconcilable to him. I now took my time, speaking very carefully and making sure he was with me every step of the way as we threaded our way through the language of sura 4:157. Then I told him about an experience I'd had a few years earlier with the president of Algeria, Abdelaziz Bouteflika, the man who had been our host when our little unofficial delegation was on its way to the Western Sahara a decade earlier.

In November 2001, I had the privilege of hosting President Bouteflika when he visited Washington. During his visit, I brought him to meet three senators in a private meeting in the congressional dining room (which, as you'll recall, was practically deserted in the post-9/11 "ghost town" months). As we sat there talking about a variety of issues, including some of our thoughts about the Jesus of the Bible and Isa of the Qur'an, one of the senators turned to Bouteflika and said, "Mr. President, I know this is an issue in Islam: what are your own thoughts about the whole matter of the Crucifixion?"

I was aghast. Here we were, talking with a Muslim president, and this American had the temerity to ask him to his face that he share his personal views on a matter that to a Muslim is an absolute heresy! Surely the senator had no idea what an offensive subject this was to bring up so casually, but nevertheless, I inwardly cringed.

But not Bouteflika. The Algerian president took it in stride, and his response was brilliant: he nodded thoughtfully and said, "Yes, well, how does one kill the eternal?" The senator had no reply.

I let Fouad absorb this vignette, then continued.

"If the man's body was crucified, as history tells us was indeed the case, then this body could not have been divine. But President Bouteflika was right, of course: you can't kill God! The *spirit* in Isa was divine, the *Ruhallah*. But on the cross he gave up that spirit. What was left was the contribution of Mary, the human part, and this part indeed died."

For a moment, we sat in silence. Then Fouad took a deep breath, turned to his wife Gina a third time, and said, "You can teach that too."

I looked at Gina and said, "Is there anything else we need to look at?"

She smiled, and for the first time during our visit, she spoke. "No, that covers everything."

I VISITED BEIRUT again a few months later, in the spring of 2006, and met Fouad and Gina at their home in the city. We went together to see Gina's boss, President Lahoud; we talked with him, shared some of our findings with him, and prayed with him for peace and reconciliation in his land. Meeting with Lahoud was a wonderful experience, but it was an even more fulfilling experience to be with this young couple again.

Although Gina had said, "That covers everything," this was not entirely the case, and we had since had a second conversation, this one walking us through an exploration of the Five Pillars of Islam and how they are at their core not in conflict with the fundamental tenets of a Christian's faith. This time it was Gina, the Christian half of this wonderful young couple, who came to a new appreciation of the accessibility of her spouse's faith.

During that visit, Gina and Fouad also took me to see a second home they were building in the coastal city of Byblos, about twenty-five miles north of Beirut. Byblos is believed to be the oldest continuously inhabited city in the world. The Greek word for "book" draws its origins from the city's name, as does our own word "Bible."

We sat on the shore of the Mediterranean and had lunch by the ocean; it was an idyllic day. The change in Gina and Fouad was heartwarming. It was clear that they were happier together and that the cloud of "religious" conflict that had settled over their marriage had completely dissipated.

As I sat on the beach with Gina and Fouad and their two young daughters, munching on falafel and cucumbers, my mind wandered back to memories of my own parents.

When I was nine, John F. Kennedy and Richard Nixon ran against each other for the highest office in the land, and politics surfaced as a mildly polarizing force among my nine-year-old friends, most of whom were only dimly becoming aware of such issues. There were Kennedy households, Nixon households— and then there was mine. We were neither. Or to put it another way, we were both.

My mother was a Democrat; my father was a Republican. One of my fondest memories is of my parents walking out the front door every election day, hand in hand, laughing and saying, "We'll be back soon, kids—we're off to the polls to cancel out each other's vote!" They were so in love. They didn't agree about politics, but they loved each other.

My wife Nancy and I are fortunate in that we see things pretty much the same way on most issues. But it certainly isn't 100 percent: there are issues we don't agree on. And between us and our four kids, there are most *certainly* things we don't agree on. Are we going to throw out our relationships because of that? Of course not. Nancy and I don't agree on everything, but we're still married. Our kids are still our kids. Not only that, we're still happy together. We don't have to see everything exactly the same way.

How much alike do we have to be before we can be friends—even close friends? My Muslim friends and I are very close; we have a bond around certain things we all feel strongly about. Yet there are a lot of things we don't agree on at all, and there are many others that we're thinking about—that we don't agree on yet, though we seem to be moving toward consensus.

Abdel would never say, for example, "Jesus was the son of God." This is far too deeply rooted a cultural heresy for most Muslims to embrace. Does he agree that Jesus was supernaturally conceived by the spirit of God through a virgin named Mary? Absolutely. Now, most Christians would say, "Yes, but that's the same thing! That means he *is* the son of God!" Well, perhaps, to them. But not to Abdel. To the two of us, this doesn't matter. We agree on what Jesus said and what he stood for, what he has to teach us and be for us today. Whether or not he died on the cross, or exactly how you frame the nature of his identity—while critical, those are separate issues.

This is an extraordinary thing, and it took a paradigm crash on both our parts to be in this place together, but here we are. Abdel is not a "casual Muslim" or wishy-washy in his beliefs; he is head of a large Muslim congregation and an influential Muslim community leader both in the United States and in his native Sudan. He is not even remotely "converted" to being a Christian.

But that's just it: *it's not "conversion" we're interested in.* It's a bond around new common ground through the transformative teachings of Jesus. It's *friendship.* True friendship doesn't demand that you be like me. True friendship asks only that you be who you are and I be who I am, and as we interact and get to know each other, that we honor and respect each other as human beings, complete in our imperfections before God.

This is not the same thing as *tolerance.* While tolerance can certainly be a good place to start, it is not enough to end there. I don't want to *tolerate* my children, I want to *love* them. Jesus never suggested that we *tolerate* our enemies. He said to *bless* them.

My parents were content to be on opposite sides of the American political spectrum and managed just fine throughout their lives. But that Republican/Democrat line of potential division was mild compared to the situation Gina and Fouad faced. They came from two opposing sides of Lebanon's Green Line, across which civil war had raged on and off for decades. And yet, as I sat with this couple, eating together on the Mediterranean shore, it could not have been more clear that their happiness together was positively transcendent. If they could find this hallowed ground, could not others find it as well?

WHEN WE RETURNED to Beirut, I met with a friend named Samir Kreidie. Samir is a prominent businessman in Lebanon who also owns a major business in Jeddah, the second largest city in Saudi Arabia. He is a Muslim follower of Jesus—a "Messianic Muslim," essentially—and a very bold, outspoken person, one of the most engaging and energetic men I know. We've been friends for years.

Samir has a beautiful penthouse home that occupies the top two floors of a beautiful fifteen-story building in downtown Beirut. A balcony wraps around it, providing breathtaking views for miles around. I could not have imagined a more evocative setting for a series of cultural summits—which is exactly what Samir had arranged. For the next few evenings, he invited the top echelon of Lebanese society to talk with me and Jim Slattery, a friend and former Democratic congressman from Kansas. One night we met the leading intellectuals, the next night the prominent politicians, and the next, the top religious leaders.

This being Beirut, these groups were of course composed of both Muslims and Christians. Conversation was lively, and with each group we shared some of our findings concerning bridges to common ground between our faiths and cultures. (The fact that Jim was a Democrat and I a Republican was not lost on anyone present, and only added to the credibility of our views.) As occurs everywhere we do this, we were met with eager fascination and people saying, "I've never thought of it that way before. . . . This is positively revolutionary!"

Meeting as we did, night after night, with this broadly varied cross section of influential figures within this diverse Middle Eastern culture, felt like a dream come true. It seemed such a clear positive indication for the future of the kind of movement we're talking about—especially in the context of Lebanon, which was where my adventures really began. Lebanon, the great experiment in Muslim-Christian coalitions; Lebanon, the cosmopolitan Paris of the Mideast; Lebanon, the place where human reason, decency, and camaraderie won out over the divisive ugliness of the Green Line.

And then it was all ripped to pieces as thirty-six days of war tore through Lebanon like a mechanized tornado from hell.

WHEN I BEGAN writing this book in the spring of 2006, I had planned to save my story of Gina and Fouad for the very end, because it is such a vignette of hope, such a beautiful microcosm of the kind of reconciliation we can and must bring about in this troubled world. When I began writing this book, Lebanon seemed the perfect place to begin the story, and the perfect place to conclude it. Lebanon was a shining example of perseverance in the pursuit of peace, and nobody exemplified this better than Gina and Fouad. Yet just a few months later, this book still in process, the beautiful city of Beirut once again lay in ruins.

During that spring 2006 visit, several months before hostilities broke out between the forces of Hezbollah and Israel, I talked with one of the top publishers in Beirut about the book I was then starting. He responded with tremendous excitement and said he intended to promote the book widely when it appeared. He said he owned three or four newspapers and magazines that he would eagerly commit to getting the word out. We had a big reception at his home with nearly a hundred people in attendance. It was a huge, gorgeous place nestled high up in the mountains overlooking Beirut.

Today the house is gone. Nothing of it remains but a charred hole in the ground.

Samir's building, thank God, was not destroyed, but with no water or power, it became impossible to continue living there. He attempted to have food and water trucked in, but there were no trucks to be found, hardly any highways, and very few standing bridges. Within days, Samir had to leave Lebanon altogether. His wife began sending me a handful of e-mails every day, full of frustration and bitterness. Samir wrote to me, "Mark, please pray for me, so that my allegiance to Jesus doesn't turn into hate."

And Gina and Fouad? They're alive and unharmed but also quite embittered.

In the aftermath of that brief but savage war, the Israeli friends I talked with all saw the conflict as entirely of Hezbollah's doing, with the support of Syria and Iran. According to my Lebanese friends, it was all the fault of Israel and, by extension, the United States. I was disheartened, though hardly surprised, to find friends on both sides locked in the same state of total intransigence, immovably committed to being right—which by definition means finding the other side wrong. This is the way it is with the human heart. It is the same for people all over the world.

Today, if I went back up into that beautiful penthouse apartment in Beirut and tried to speak with those same groups, we wouldn't be able to have a conversation. The guests would yell and scream and pound their fists.

•   •   •

THAT FALL, MANY of my friends asked me if this setback had discouraged me or in any way dimmed my hope for the future. My answer was and is, "No—quite the opposite." Of course it saddened me immensely to see such great progress and positivity turned senselessly into rubble. And this was not some vague CNN reportage to me—these were my friends. But every new disastrous, destructive development makes what we're doing *more* important, not less.

Am I made less hopeful with each new eruption of hostilities, each new incidence of suicide bombings, each fresh escalation in the seemingly interminable cycle of attack and retribution? Quite the opposite: I'm *more* hopeful. My friends and I are not the only ones who know that the situation has to change and that it is up to private individuals, not governments, to change it. As much as division and hatred is endemic to the human heart, even more is hope and striving for peace part and parcel of the human spirit.

In his best-selling book *The Tipping Point* (2000), Malcolm Gladwell gives a penetrating analysis of what he calls "social epidemics," instances when an idea has gone raging through a society every bit as contagiously as a disease. In both cases, says Gladwell, the precise same conditions and characteristics apply. The book brilliantly explores the critical factors involved: the *infectious agent* itself; the *carriers* or *highly influential people* who transmit the infectious agent; and the *medium* or *receptive environment* through which the infectious agent spreads.[1]

In our case, the infectious agent is an idea: the radical idea of reconciliation that Jesus taught two millennia ago and, in my view, that the Qur'an reiterated. The highly influential carriers are people like ourselves, those handfuls of individuals in each community who are befriending and influencing the opinion-leaders. And the medium or receptive environment is a world community increasingly alarmed by the growing gulf between East and West that every day becomes a more terrifying chasm aching to be bridged.

As tragic as the Israeli-Lebanese war was, it also served to force people on both sides into a position of more openness. In the wake of this and every new conflict, more and more people are asking, "Okay—what do we do now?" People are looking for answers. And not just a few people, but people the world over.

When at home in Virginia, I watch Middle Eastern programming on satellite television every chance I get, from as many as a dozen countries. Both from the international media and from my own travels, it's abundantly clear to me that Islam itself is going through a period of deep reflection. Their term for this type of profound and open-minded reconsideration of an issue is *Ijtihad*, a technical term of Islamic law that was discarded nine hundred years ago in favor of more conservative stances, but which now appears to be undergoing a renaissance. Perhaps Islam is going through a cycle similar to that of Christianity during its two-thousand-year history.

The people of the world, both East and West, are doing some serious soul-searching about the nature and meaning of Islam and its relationship with the rest of the world community, and this is exactly the kind of careful self-reflection needed on both sides of the East-West divide.

It's easy to let the saber-rattling and chest-beating of ideologues, political leaders, and other polarizing public spokespeople on every side distract us, but their polemics provide no solid answers. The answers will required nothing less than a spiritual revolution, a revolution without guns and tanks, a revolution of the human heart. While it may seem impossible to some, I have become convinced that it is not. Indeed, it is more *possible* now than ever before. It is likely the greatest challenge, and the greatest opportunity, of the twenty-first century.

SEVENTEEN

Path of Peace
in a Time of War

How, then? If this revolution of the human heart is to happen, if it is indeed possible, then *how* will it happen? What do we need to do?

The first thing is to recognize what it is we're dealing with. The forces of anti-Western Muslim terrorism are not a centralized, hierarchical organization that we can conquer by fighting it head-on in classic military style. What we're dealing with is not an organization but a *movement*. A movement is not organized along classic centralized lines, with a central authority at the hub and a hierarchy of minions who execute the commands of the chief. It follows an entirely different set of rules.

In their book *The Starfish and the Spider*, Stanford researchers Ori Brafman and Rod A. Beckstrom compare centralized structures—such as a classic kingdom, conventional army, or twentieth-century corporation—to a spider: cut off its head and the legs die. But a starfish has no "head." Cut off one of its legs and it will simply grow a new one. Not only that, but the leg you just cut off will also *grow a new starfish*.[1]

The Internet is a good example of a starfish, say Brafman and Beckstrom, and so is Alcoholics Anonymous. So is the open-source software movement. And so is al-Qaeda.

If there is no centralized authority or hierarchy, then how does a decentralized movement get and stay organized? What keeps it going? Understand the answer to that question, and we have a place to start.

Such organic, person-to-person organizations are bound together and driven by a *passionately shared belief.* It is not an authoritarian chain of command, held together by a central office or individual authority, that holds decentralized organizations together, but *ideology.* And the ideology that coheres al-Qaeda and their far-flung network of tiny cell groups, the driving force that keeps the engine of terrorism going, is the idea that Western civilization is bent on militarily overrunning the Muslim world, as exemplified by the United States' unbending support for Israel, and that the only way to fight back is through a so-called jihad of holy war and its secret weapon, terrorist martyrdom fueled by a virtually endless stream of recruits.

We cannot make any genuine, lasting progress in the "war on terror" without understanding this fundamental truth about the force that is challenging the West. We have to understand that *ideology*—not political power, military might, or economic resources—is the cohesive force that holds a movement like Muslim militancy together. Ideology is its strength—and its weakness. No military force on earth can defeat an ideology bound together by passion. And therein lies the answer: if you can effectively find a flaw in its ideology and widely expose that flaw, you crack apart the organization's coherence.

Unfortunately, the strategy many in the West are now following accomplishes precisely the opposite result. For example, as I pointed out in an earlier chapter, the term "jihad" has been hijacked to serve the ends of militant extremists. Every time we in the West use the militants' vocabulary to describe them, we are putting our tacit stamp of approval on their twisting of their own scriptures. Use their terms, and we're making their case for them! And this is not a purely semantic distinction; we are dealing here with ideology, which is the lifeblood of the movement.

One of the overarching goals of the Muslim militants' master strategies is to forge one gigantic Islamic state under sharia law, transcending current national boundaries and placing all infidels in subjugation. There is a bizarre irony here, because pursuing such an imperialistic impulse is exactly what they accuse the West of doing, though the ranks of followers don't seem to notice this glaring contradiction.

In truth, this goal takes quite a leap of the imagination: the Muslim populations of the East are extremely diverse and as far from a unified bloc as one could imagine. Still, nothing unites feuding parties like a common enemy, and it is in vilifying the West that ideologues such as bin Laden hope to bring about that unity. Even so, it's quite a tall order. It's a lot easier to terrorize a perceived enemy through random acts of violence than it is to forge a lasting unity among such divergent and fractious groups as those in the Middle East, and the bin Ladens of the movement have little to offer in that direction but empty rhetoric.

We should be pointing all this out. Instead, the leading voices in the West continue to make public pronouncements about the "global Islamicist network" that serve only to lend credibility to the extremists' imperialistic goals. As *Newsweek* columnist Fareed Zakaria puts it:

The White House is lumping Chechen separatists in Russia, Pakistani-backed militants in India, Shi'ite politicians in Iraq and Sunni jihadists in Egypt all together as one worldwide movement. This is, of course, exactly what bin Laden has argued all along. But why is Bush making bin Laden's case?[2]

It's not only the ideologues' nation-building political agenda that our rhetoric supports; more importantly, by our reactions we are feeding into the *religious ideology* that drives the movement itself. Angrily railing against Muslim terrorism actually supports and feeds it. When Christian leaders say that Muhammad was a mass murderer, that the Qur'an promotes violence, that Islam is all about destroying the Western way of life . . . well, none of these statements is technically true—but they are exactly what the Muslim militants are telling their millions of followers!

Remember, like the soldiers of the Crusades, the overwhelming majority of these people cannot read or understand their holy books for themselves. They rely on their spiritual leaders for translation and interpretation. These vulnerable, impressionable young men and women are being told that they should martyr themselves because there's no other hope of salvation or way to defend the Islamic way of life threatened by Western decadence, and that the surest, purest, most martyrdom-worthy cause is the destruction of infidels. This message is slowly penetrating even the literate upper classes of Islamic society. By affirming this nefarious militant ideology, we only perpetuate it.

What should we do instead? Rather than supporting that ideology, we need to confront it, challenge it, and expose it as the profoundly flawed, manipulative misrepresentation it is. Those Muslim leaders joining this movement to counter radicalism need to stand up and say, "No, I'm sorry, the Qur'an does *not* say that. This is a text that more than one billion people say is the word of God—and you're misinterpreting and twisting it. You're wrong, and we can prove it to you by reading the original language."

These efforts must be led by Muslims and supported by those of us in the West who can educate our own and help to lift the veil of ignorance that continues to fuel this deadly misunderstanding.

In 2003, a young Yemeni judge named Hamoud al-Hitar did exactly that. Entering Yemen's Sanaa prison with a group of four other Islamic scholars, he met with five incarcerated al-Qaeda militants and gave them a challenge: "If you can convince us that your ideas are justified in the Qur'an, then we will join your struggle; but if we succeed in convincing you of our ideas, then you must renounce violence." Two years later, the five were out of prison and promoting peace—along with 359 others who had followed suit.[3]

The story of the judge's courageous action held a special layer of meaning to me: it was strangely reminiscent of Doug's challenging me to find a scriptural basis for my policy of converting nonbelievers.

We need to remember that an ideology is more than just an *opinion* or *viewpoint*; it is a deeply, passionately, firmly held set of beliefs. An ideology does not change by increments or through mild suggestion; it is a dramatic and profound change of heart and mind we're talking about. When I experienced my own personal paradigm crash in the late 1980s, my ideology changed. My worldview didn't just shift—it cracked and split apart. And that's precisely what's needed here: not simply to *influence* people's thinking, but to profoundly *alter* it at its core.

"FINE," SAYS THE skeptic, "but how? How can one possibly organize a campaign massive enough to change the ideologies of enough people to actually turn the tide of Muslim militancy around the globe?" One answer is, *by being organically decentralized ourselves.*

The way you change a decentralized movement is by changing its ideology; and the way you can most effectively do that is by being an organic, person-to-person movement yourself. How does one organize such a movement? The same way every effective movement in history has done it: in small, informal, spontaneous "core circles" of a few individuals each. The strategy here is to find the influential people, the opinion-leaders in every community, the key businessmen, religious leaders, politicians, media people, anyone with broad influence over those segments of their community; and once we've found them, to befriend them, talk with them, show them the common ground that exists between our faiths and cultures, change their understanding.

Just as this deadly misunderstanding is mutual, so is the transformation that leads to its resolution. That transformation must come from those of both East and West. If this new understanding were embraced in both Muslim and Christian communities around the world, can you imagine what would happen?

We *know* because it's already happening.

ON A TRIP to Sudan's capital city of Khartoum in 2006, I went with a small group to attend a prayer service at a large mosque in the heart of the city. The group consisted of my friends Abdel and Bill, myself, and a few American Christian friends; aside from Abdel, we all felt distinctly conspicuous as the service got under way. In fact, the word "conspicuous" doesn't even begin to describe how out of place we felt in this magnificently ornate house of Islamic worship. Picture a lone knot of Arab Muslims standing in the middle of the Christian throng at Sunday mass at St. Patrick's, then add the fact that Sudan is one of the few countries on the globe with whom the United States has no diplomatic relations, and you begin to get a sense of it.

"I'll bet this doesn't happen very often," I whispered to our Sudanese host. "You know, Christian Westerners at Friday afternoon prayers in Khartoum."

"No," he whispered back. "Not so often. First time."

As guest imam, Abdel stood to present the sermon. He spoke for a minute about how the two of us had met in the months immediately after 9/11, pointing out that if that meeting had been twenty years earlier, when I was a brash young Christian Republican congressman and he an outspoken young Sudanese Muslim law student, we would have been unable to see each other as anything but "the enemy." He described to the crowd the impossible distances we had each traveled, both in our minds and in our hearts, to arrive at a place where we could form these bonds of friendship, and he briefly chronicled some of our efforts to help build bridges between East and West. He said he hoped the congregation would give his American friends a hearing, and then turned the floor over to me.

Standing to face a thousand Muslims assembled in their place of worship, I spoke these words in Arabic: "In the name of God most merciful and compassionate, peace be with you. I am here to speak with you about bridges to the common ground."

For the next few minutes, I spoke about pathways to peace and reconciliation, about the Qur'an and the Bible and some of the startling areas of overlap and commonality between Islam and Christianity, two faiths supposedly locked in irreconcilable conflict. I explained that our sole objective was to help build bridges of better understanding between our cultures, and that for all our differences, there is a good deal more that we share than most of us have been led to believe.

After we finished speaking, we were mobbed by what seemed like the entire assembly. They crowded around us by the hundreds, saying, "May Allah bless you. . . . Thank you for everything you're doing. . . . We want peace with America." Abdel's face beamed in an ear-to-ear grin as we made our way through the crowd. Phil Sheldon, a right-wing Evangelical Christian who was part of our group, was so moved he was weeping.

And this scenario is only a tiny microcosm of what is taking place around the world.

Indonesia is the largest Muslim-majority nation in the world; Bangladesh is the third largest; in both countries, there is a huge

"Messianic Muslim" movement—that is, people who are Muslims, not Christians; who worship at mosques, not churches; who pray on carpets, not in pews; who faithfully follow the Five Pillars of Islam and all the cultural and traditional aspects of their faith—and have fully embraced the teachings and person of Jesus.

While I refer to these people as "Messianic Muslims," this is not how they identify themselves.[4] They retain their cultural identity, they go to the mosque and read the Qur'an, *and* they pray in the name of Jesus and read the Bible. They make every effort to be as normal as possible and not stand out. In too many of these societies, converting to another religion is an infraction punishable by death.

And even if this were not so, why should they make such a claim anyway? These people aren't "converting" or forsaking their traditions, cultures, or families, let alone Islam or the Qur'an. It's just that they're embracing Jesus in a new way. They aren't leaving anything behind. They're simply discovering a powerful new common ground.

A CHRISTIAN MISSIONARY once went to a Muslim village in the mostly Muslim West African nation of Mali. He told the people there about Jesus, but he was careful to show them the Jesus of the Qur'an. The whole village came to Jesus, as the expression goes, and embraced Isa al-Masih wholeheartedly. At the same time, they continued going to their mosque and maintaining their Sunni Muslim traditions.

The village flourished.

Eventually, the missionary left. Soon a new Christian missionary came and saw what the villagers were doing. He said, "Oh no, you can't have a mosque. You need a church!" So they built a church, with beautiful wooden pews and wonderful stained glass.

Within five years, the church was abandoned and the whole town fell into a mess.

This is the tragic misunderstanding and arrogance of our Western concept of "conversion." True religion is a *state of being*. According to James, it is "helping the widows and orphans, and keeping yourself pure within the world." According to the Qur'an, it is *deen*, being completely indebted to God.

What are purity and total submission to God? They are both *states of being*. And this is precisely what Abdel and I and our friends are talking about: a worldwide movement, based on a state of being, not membership in a "club." We don't want anyone to convert *from* anything or *to* anything. What we're after is *shalem*: reconciliation, resolution, peace.

CHANGING THE WORLD can seem like a daunting task, but the truth is, those movements and revolutions that have changed the world have always started with nothing but a handful of people (like Jesus and his twelve) who earnestly seek the different world that such a movement would bring about. In the United States, there are perhaps a dozen political leaders who profoundly mold the thinking of millions of citizens, and no more than fifteen well-placed Christian leaders who frame the fundamental impressions of a hundred million churchgoers.

In 1999, Pope John Paul II caused quite a stir when, at the conclusion of an audience with some representatives of both Sunni and Shi'ite groups, he was given a copy of the Qur'an as a gift— and as a sign of respect toward the holy book, he bowed to it and kissed it. His successor, Benedict XVI, has been viewed as being less sanguine on this subject. In September 2006 (one day after the fifth anniversary of 9/11) he stirred up controversy and anger among Muslims by quoting a fourteenth-century emperor's view that Islam is "evil and inhuman" and intrinsically linked with violence. There are about 1.2 billion Catholics in the world; even the most conservative estimate suggests that at least a few hundred million are profoundly influenced when the pope speaks. And when Franklin Graham declared in the fall of 2001 that Islam is "a very evil and wicked religion,"[5] there were probably hundreds of millions of Christians throughout the world who believed him, too. Isn't that amazing: two people speak, and hundreds upon hundreds of millions of people follow.

It is always thus: a small handful of people truly committed to their cause hold sway over the views, beliefs, and actions of millions. *And a core of just a few, equally committed to their cause, have the very real potential to reach and influence those key leaders.*

In the Middle East and North Africa, there are arguably thirty key Muslim clerics who hold the power to influence the vast majority of Islam's followers, including many hundreds of millions in Islamic Asia. There are fifty-two countries with sizable Muslim populations; more than half of them (probably thirty-one of the fifty-two) are primarily Islamic. In other words, in each of these countries there are but a handful of religious extremists who exert powerful sway over those most susceptible to enlistment into martyrdom—that's *one or two hundred people.* That's it.

We cannot beat these people with armies—but we can take away their power. How? By challenging their ideology. By creating a paradigm crash with an ideologically decentralized movement of our own, composed of people who genuinely seek peace and are willing to pursue it by engaging in the radical teaching of the Sermon on the Mount—not just paying it lip service but actually *living* it. People who are willing to love their enemies. My friends and I believe there is at least a handful of such people in every city in the world. In every community, there are but a handful of influential trouble-makers—and they can be reached through a handful of influential peacemakers.

Obviously the U.S. Congress is an imperfect community; indeed, it is one of our greatest lightning rods for scandal and popular discontent. Yet some wonderful things are happening in Congress, not least the informal prayer groups that now comprise nearly one-fourth of both chambers, working to build stronger ties with each other and with others around the world on a basis of friendship, and to seek out the commonalities that bring us together rather than emphasizing the differences that divide us.

Through the work of these groups, wonderful reconciliations have occurred. Even bipartisan legislation has been introduced as a result of friendships made at the breakfasts. And similar fellowship groups now exist in the parliaments of perhaps a hundred other countries. Some of them are more overtly religious than others, some more widespread and some more locally based, but they all are creating networks of devoted friends who believe passionately in the same goal: to establish peace through organic, personal relationships—yes, even with our worst enemies.

I've shared in these pages a few brief examples of the kinds of experiences we've had in hot spots around the world in pursuit of this sort of "friendship diplomacy." We have had dozens and dozens of similar experiences—and so have many others. These networked groups are already having an impact in parliaments and palaces, cabals and cabinets, all over the globe. We don't need millions or thousands. We only need a handful in every community.

People ask, "How many years will it take to build this peaceful, paradigm-crashing movement you're talking about?" It could happen in *months*.

OVER THE LAST few years, I have had the opportunity to spend some time with two former prime ministers of Somalia, a nearly 100 percent Muslim country so torn apart by its warring clans that it hasn't had a functioning central government since

1991. Their comments echoed the same thoughts: as one lamented, since civil war seized his country in the late 1980s, there had been endless division, lawlessness, and interminable violence. He was now in the United States, he said, on a mission to find some kind of solution to his people's seemingly interminable crisis.

I asked him what he thought was at the root of the problems in Somalia. Was it a religious division?

"No," he replied, "we are all Muslims."

Did he think it came down to a conflict based on ethnicity?

"No," he repeated, "we are all essentially the same ethnic background."

Was it tribal? He shook his head. Cultural? He sighed, and shook his head again. Grasping at straws, I asked if there were differences in language or dialect?

"No," he said, "we mostly all speak the same language."

Why would the Somali people stay so alienated for so long, and over what? What would drive the rage, mistrust, and wanton killing of neighbors and friends if they are all essentially the same people? As we talked, the prime minister and I came to the same conclusion: the center of the problem was simply the dark side of human nature.

While this book focuses on bridges between the Muslim East and Christian West, the issue at its core is humanity's historic compulsion to be at war with itself. Our excuses for war are endless, but the truth is that war and conflict, division and mutual hostility need no more basis than the stubborn human tendency that is forever splitting our world into bitterly opposed camps. Whether Arab against Arab (Iraq), Christian against Christian (Northern Ireland), or Arab, Christian, and Jew against each other (Lebanon), it is at its core the same conflict. Beirut's Green Line, Korea's 38th Parallel, Germany's Berlin Wall, the United States' Mason-Dixon Line, and all the hundreds of thousands of similar partitions that we have erected throughout history and around the globe—they are all echoes of the same barren line of separation within the human heart, the same deadly misunderstanding.

In ancient Egypt, the heart was considered the seat of thought and emotion, and was the only organ not removed during mummification. The heart is mentioned in the Bible more than any other topic, and is discussed more than 150 times in the Qur'an.

"If we could just find a way to influence the human heart to love rather than to hate," said my Somali friend, "then there may be hope for Somalia."

Indeed, if we can find a way to do this, then there is hope for the rest of the world as well.

The concepts Jesus taught are as radical today as they were two thousand years ago, because they run counter to our divisive human nature—a nature that is perennially finding new Green Lines to create and then shooting across them at each other. It seems clear to me that these concepts represent the only hope of bridging the Muslim-Christian divide and subduing the shrill escalation of rhetoric, resentment, and retribution between East and West. We know that most foreign ministries and formal diplomatic bodies (certainly including the U.S. Department of State) will not likely engage a policy of "loving" their enemies. But *you and I* can do exactly that.

How do we do this? What does this kind of love look like? Again, Paul's first letter to his little community in Corinth provides a vivid picture of both what this kind of love is *not* (envious, boastful, proud, focused on its own agenda, readily provoked, always keeping a tally of the other's wrongs, or relishing trouble and misfortune) and also what it *is:* patient, kind, truthful, protecting, trusting, hopeful, enduring, and, finally, consistent and never-failing. I have witnessed firsthand how friendships based on these aspects of love can yield power beyond imagination, penetrating the hearts of even the most hardened despot.

Can we do this? Of course we can, and we *must*. The alternative is to do nothing and see our world consumed by an irrational maelstrom of hatred and violence.

And now, the real question: Can *you* do this?

I believe you can. I know I am a work in progress, and I'm sure you are as well; we all are. Yet in my own life, I've been amazed to see how far this transformation can go, both within my own heart and in the hearts of those to whom I have reached out. And now I reach out to you, with this simple challenge: that you adopt this radical, contrarian message as your own. Peace in the world will never be born in the halls of congresses and parliaments, in disarmament conferences or treaty negotiations. It is conceived and nourished in the hearts of singular men and women, committed to extinguishing the potential perils that face our children and grandchildren, through the unrelenting generosity of our own spirits.

It is only through building organic, individual friendships that the dark passions of hate, revenge, bitterness, and greed can be softened and transformed into love, forgiveness, and peace. It is only through such acts of friendship that our deadliest misunderstandings can be put behind us, and we can genuinely begin to bridge the Muslim-Christian divide.

"Love your enemy." What a mind-boggling, heart-transforming idea. Making friends with the people you thought you hated. It's that radical, that simple, and that necessary.

> For if you forgive men their faults, your Father in heaven will also forgive you. (Matt. 6:14)

> If a person forgives and makes reconciliation, his reward is due from Allah. (sura 42:40)

Salaam; shlama; shalom.

Jesus in the Qur'an

A Complete List of Qur'anic References to Isa (Jesus)

Isa spoke from Mary's womb: *5:110, 19:24, 19:29–33.*

Isa was conceived supernaturally through a virgin named Mary; spoken into being [*faya kun*] and by the breath or spirit of Allah [*Ruh al-qudis Allah*] or Holy Spirit: *2:87, 2:253, 3:47, 3:59, 5:110, 19:20 ff, 21:29, 66:12.*

Isa is of Allah's Spirit [*Ruh ana Allah*]: *19:17, 21:29, 21:91, 66:12.*

Isa is a Spirit of/from Allah [*Ruh minhu* from *Allah*]: *4:171.*

Isa, a son pure, without sin [*zakiyyah*]: *3:38, 19:19.*

Isa had no vanity or wickedness: *19:32.*

Isa is righteous [*saliheen*]: *3:46, 6:85.*

Isa called the messiah: *3:45, 4:157, 4:171, 4:172, 5:17 (twice), 5:72 (twice), 5:75, 9:30, 9:31.*

Isa is the gospel or good news: *3:45.*

Isa is considered a mediator [*wajih*; other than in reference to Moses, this is the only use of the term *wajih* in the entire Qur'an]: *3:45.*

Isa as intercessor [*shafa'a*; this is as an exclusive right of Allah, who may pass it down to whomever he likes]: *2:255, 21:28.*

Isa is noble [*wagihan*] now and hereafter [*wagihn* or *wajih* also means "noble and exalted"]: *6:85.*

Isa breathed life into clay: *3:49, 5:110.*

Isa the word of Allah [*kalimat Allah*]: *3:39, 3:45, 4:171.*

Isa the word of truth: *19:34.*

Isa the tidings of things unseen (supernatural): *3:44.*

Only two things sent from heaven, Isa and the Holy Book: *5:15, 5:114, 5:115.*

Isa strengthened/led [*ayyada*] by the Holy Spirit [*Ruh Qudus*]: *2:87, 2:253, 5:110.*

Allah's favor was on him [Isa]: *43:59, 5:110.*

Isa was given revelation from Allah: *2:136, 3:59, 19:30.*

Allah revealed his will to Isa: *4:163.*

Isa a mercy from Allah: *19:21.*

Isa had power to raise the dead: *3:49, 5:110.*

Isa a clear sign [*be-yinat*, meaning "clear and without doubt"] unto men (all mankind): *2:87, 3:49–50, 5:115, 19:21, 21:93, 43:61.*

Isa showed clear signs [*be-yinat*] of Allah: *2:253, 5:110, 43:63.*

Allah gave clear miracles to Isa: *2:253.*

Isa healed the sick and lepers: *3:49, 5:110.*

Isa died [*mutawafeka*, rooted in *wafat* and *amutu*]: *3:55, 4:159, 5:117, 19:33.*

Isa resurrected from the dead [*yum uba'athu*]: *2:72–73, 19:33.*

Isa present at Resurrection Day [*yum al-qiyama*]: *3:55, 4:159.*

Isa ascended up to Allah in heaven: *3:55, 4:158.*

Isa coming back to judge the world: *3:55, 4:159, 4:173, 43:61.*

Isa a sign of the hour of judgment: *43:61.*

Isa near to Allah [*mugarrabeen*, a special place of honor]: *3:45.*

Allah blessed Isa wherever he was: *19:31.*

Isa given wisdom of the Old Testament and gospel: *3:48, 3:110, 19:30.*

Isa had the favor of Allah: *43:59.*

Isa a servant and prophet of Allah: *4:172, 19:30.*

Isa miraculously brings food to earth from heaven: *5:112–118.*

Isa a straight (right) path: *43:61.*

Isa a witness for Allah: *4:159, 5:117.*

Allah made a covenant with Isa: *33:7*.

Isa an apostle: *4:157, 4:71, 5:75*.

Isa an example to the children of Israel: *43:59*.

Angels near to Isa: *4:172*.

Isa coming to attest the law: *3:50*.

Isa like (is the second) Adam: *3:59*.

Isa is the right path to follow: *43:61*.

Isa inspired disciples [*al-hawariyun*] to have faith in Allah: *5:111*.

Disciples of Isa have power over their enemies: *61:14*.

We are ordered to obey Isa: *3:50, 4:159, 5:111, 43:61, 43:63*.

Isa came with wisdom (authority) of Allah: *43:63*.

Ordered to follow Isa: *3:44, 43:61*.

Followers of Isa superior: *3:55*.

Disciples are Allah's helpers of the revelation of Isa: *3:52, 61:14*.

Disciples are witnesses to the truth of Isa: *5:113*.

Followers of Isa acceptable (true believers) to Allah: *18:10, 57:27, 85:4*.

Linguistic Similarities

Key Terms in Hebrew, Aramaic, and Arabic

English	Hebrew	Aramaic	Arabic
peace, surrender (etc.)	shalom	shlama	salaam
"Peace be with you"	shalom alechum	shlama lokh	salam a laek
God	Eloah (Elohim)	Alaha	Allah
Spirit of God	Ruah ha Elohem	Rohka Alaha	Ruh Allah
Holy Spirit	Ruah ha Kadoish	Rohka d'Qudsha	Ruh al-Qudus
Jesus	Yeshuah	Eshoo / Yeshuah	Isa / Issa
Messiah	Meshiach	Meshikha	Masih
proclaim, testify	shema / hagah	sahda	shahada
pray	tephillah	saalee / slotha	salah
giving	tzsedhagah	leeyawa	zakat
fasting	tsuwm	soma	sawm
pilgrimage	khawgog	habo	hajj
struggle	abaq	ji'ah	jihad
religion	(*no equivalent*)	deenaa / dilath	deen
begat	yâlad	yalad	yalad
born of	yalad	yalad	walada / maoulood
only son	ykhiaday	yachidaya	eyal / waheed
angel	malacha	maalaakha	mala'ika
hell	gehenna / sheol	gehenna	jahanam / jehannam

Examples of Aramaic Terms That Clarify Long-standing Biblical Misinterpretations

In chapter 3 we detail several examples where the Aramaic terms of the Peshitta version of the New Testament clear up long-standing textual puzzles and misinterpretations. The examples there involved the passages "It is easier for a camel to go through the eye of a needle than for a rich man to enter the kingdom of God" and "If anyone comes to me and does not hate his father and mother . . . he cannot be my disciple." Both passages were found to be garbled versions of the original intent—and in each case it was a single Aramaic term that provided the solution to the riddle. This same process occurs over and over in the New Testament; one of the most critical examples is the handful of words typically translated as "convert," as the balance of that chapter explains.

Here are further examples of passages where Aramaic, the "secret language of the Bible," provides valuable clarification and sorts out long-held misunderstandings.

Does God Tempt Us or Not?

Of all the apparent contradictions in the text of the Bible, none is more intriguing than instances where Jesus's own words appear to contain contradictory teachings. One such example occurs in the wording of the famous Lord's Prayer, the prayer Jesus taught his followers in Matthew 6:9–13. The problematic passage is the prayer's concluding words: "And do not lead us into temptation, but deliver us from the evil one" (Matt. 6:13, NKJV).

Here is the issue: In James 1:14 the New Testament says, "Let no man say, when he is tempted, I am tempted by God, for God cannot be tempted with evil; neither does he tempt any man." But if it's true that God never tempts us, why would Jesus instruct us to pray that God not lead us into temptation?

The Aramaic Peshitta text corrects this substantial inconsistency: "And do not *let* us enter into temptation, but deliver us from evil" (emphasis added).[1]

Did Jesus Really Say, "I Come to Bring a Sword"?

"Do not suppose I have come to bring peace on earth; I have not come to bring peace but a sword" (Matt. 10:34). At first blush, this verse seems to contradict all of Jesus's teachings. How could the man who taught us to "turn the other cheek" and "love our enemies" claim that he came to bring a sword? In fact, this verse has even been used by some to justify violence against "nonbelievers."

The truer meaning here is not sword, but *division*. This is more accurately rendered in the common English translations of the corresponding passage in Luke: "Do you think I have come to bring peace on earth? I say to you, No, but divisions" (Luke 12:51).

The teachings of Jesus were so revolutionary and contrary to the political, social, and religious order of the day that when people followed them, divisions among families, friends, and institutions inevitably ensued. Dr. Lamsa comments that the Greeks did not understand the Eastern idiomatic aspect of these verses. Jesus never suggested that his followers ought to "take up the sword," but meant rather that following him would inevitably cause "divisions" and persecutions—as history has in fact shown to be the case.

"Let the Dead Bury the Dead"

This is one of those problematic verses that can lead to some fairly tortured interpretation in the effort to make sense out of it. Spoken by Jesus in Matthew 8:21–22, this statement does seem confusing when taken at face value: how can the dead bury the dead? Sometimes this is interpreted to mean that those who are "spiritually dead" should be left to bury the physically dead.

The Aramaic suggests a more straightforward explanation. Dr. Lamsa points out that the first Aramaic word for "dead" in this verse is *medita,* which also means "town," while the second "dead" is *metta.* The two terms, he argues, are so similar in "formation and pronunciation . . . that it is possible that an error occurred during copying." The verse may simply mean, "Follow me and let the townspeople bury their dead."

Are Women Really Weaker in the Bible?

Much has been written about presumed biblical attitudes toward women, and this is an area that is rich in examples of mistranslation or cultural misinterpretation. One prominent example is 1 Peter 3:7, which suggests that husbands should treat their wives as the weaker partner ("weaker vessel," in NKJV). This verse has been taken by many as providing scriptural authority for the idea that women are "weaker" or somehow inferior to men.

The Eastern text again brings clarity to a deeply held misunderstanding: the Aramaic version says, "Husbands, . . . hold them with tenderness like delicate [fragile] vessels," suggesting that women are to be honored, respected, held in high esteem, and treated as such.

Is Joseph the Father of Jesus?

The very opening of the New Testament produces an apparent contradiction that Muslims often point to as proof of the Injil's corruption: Matthew says that Joseph—not God—is Jesus's father! The first seventeen verses of the Gospel according to Matthew traces the entire genealogy, from Abraham to Jesus—and the detailed genealogy ends with "and Jacob begot Joseph, the husband of Mary, of whom was born Jesus, who is called Christ."

Joseph? If Jesus was spiritually conceived—which both the Bible and the Qur'an affirm—then what is Joseph doing in his genealogy?

"It's bad enough," I've been told on more than one occasion, "that Christians say that Isa is Allah's 'begotten son,'"—this misunderstanding is explained in chapter 12—"but then your own Bible contradicts it!"

Or does it?

Actually, there is a second problem in this passage: after tracing the entire genealogy from Abraham to Jesus, verse 17 sums up by referring to three sets of fourteen generations: "Therefore all the generations from Abraham to David are fourteen generations; and from David to the Babylonian captivity are fourteen generations; and from the Babylonian captivity to Christ are fourteen generations."

But when one actually counts out that third set of generations, Joseph is only number twelve, which would make Jesus number thirteen—not fourteen. A blatant contradiction of its own math!

Once again, Aramaic provides the answer to this riddle, and it solves both problems with a single word. The Aramaic word here translated as "husband" is *gowra*. Yet only several verses later, when Matthew refers to "Joseph her husband," the text uses a different Aramaic word, *baalah*, which also means "husband." Why use two different terms in the span of only three verses? Because the text is referring to two different people.

The earlier term, *gowra*, has several other meanings, including "head of the household" and "father." Joseph was as common a name in first-century Israel as it is in contemporary America. The Joseph of the genealogy was not Mary's husband, but Mary's father—same name, different man.[2]

Thus, Jacob (generation #11) had a son named Joseph (generation #12) who had a daughter named Mary (generation #13)—who miraculously conceived and bore a son named Jesus: generation #14.

•   •   •

For further study, please see the following interesting comparisons of the phrases from the Greek side by side with the same phrases from the Aramaic translations:

English (NIV) from Greek	**English (Peshitta) from the Aramaic**
	Aramaic terms, where available, in italics
Matt. 5:3	
poor in spirit	humble [*miskene bruh*]
Matt. 5:22	
(no Greek version: Aramaic quoted within the Greek text)	I spit on you! [*Raca!*]
Matt. 5:29	
If your right eye causes you to sin, gouge it out.	Eliminate bad visions from your eyes.
Matt. 5:39	
If someone strikes you on the right cheek, turn to him the other also.	Do not start a quarrel or fight. Be humble.
	[*Illa man dmahe lakh al Pakakh dyammeena: Apna leh ap Hrena*]
Matt. 6:3	
Do not let your left hand know what your right hand is doing.	Do not advertise your giving.
	[*La thidda simmalakh mana avda yammeenakh*]
Matt. 7:6	
Do not throw your pearls to swine.	Do not use wise sayings before fools.
	[*marganyathkhon qdam hsiere*]
Matt. 10:16	
wise as serpents	avoid trouble [*khakkieme akh khvavatha*]
Matt. 10:16	
harmless as doves	trustful, pure in heart [*thammime akh yavne*]
Matt. 10:34	
to bring a sword	to bring division

Matt. 10:38
take up the cross

risk the life, willing to die [*shaquel zqiepe*]

Matt. 16:18
upon this rock (or stone)

upon this truth [*al hade kepa*]

Matt. 18:19
if two of you shall agree

if two of you are worthy

Matt. 19:24
camel through the eye of a needle

rope [*gamla,* thick thread] through the eye of the needle

Matt. 20:15
is thy eye evil

envious, jealous [*av ainakh bisha*]

Matt. 20:23
you shall drink of my cup

die as I die [*kas tishton*]

Matt. 27:46
My God, my God,
why has thou forsaken me?

My God, my God,
this is my destiny.
[*Eli Eli lemana shabakthani*]

Mark 16:18
take up a serpent

handle an enemy, overcome opposition

Mark 16:18
drink any deadly thing

martyrdom

Luke 3:5
crooked places made straight

crooked teachings replaced by the truth

Luke 5:39
old and new wine

Judaism and Jesus's teaching

Luke 9:27
shall not taste of death

shall not die spiritually
[*la nithemuv mautha*]

Luke 10:19
tread on serpents

to overcome enemies and opposition
[*daishin khwawatha*]

Luke 12:49
come to bring fire on the earth

upset the order of the day,
revolutionizing the world

John 1:18
the only begotten son

born only of a woman
[hence, a spiritual son of God]

John 3:3
born again

to become like a child,
to start all over [*mithielid min dresh*]

John 14:2
in my Father's house are many
rooms

a kingdom for all races and people

John 21:15
Feed my lambs. [Jesus to Peter]

Feed my young people,
take care of them.

John 21:16
Feed my sheep. [Jesus to Peter]

Feed the adults.

John 21:17
Feed my ewes. [Jesus to Peter]

Feed the young women.

Acknowledgments

I am in debt to my infinitely supportive family: to my wife, Nancy, who has partnered with me through all the research, listened to my lectures for hours, sat through countless meetings and gone on innumerable trips, welcomed guests in our home from all over the world, and helped improve my writings with her consummate editorial skills; and to our four children, Elizabeth, Laura Ashley, Allison Marie, and Mark Jr., who have each in his or her own way championed this work over the years; and my brother Bill, and sisters Eva and Susan. This book is about learning to love one another despite our differences, and at times *because* of our differences. Nowhere have I learned that lesson of compassion and humility more deeply than here at home from my wonderful family.

I must also express deep appreciation for a number of dear friends who have in one way or another contributed to the motivation, inspiration, and technical aspects of this book. In alphabetic order:

William Aramony, for his strategic advice, partnership, and travel companionship.

Imam Abdel Azim, for his patient instruction on the Qur'an and Arabic language and his demonstration that the gulf can be bridged in friendship.

Rev. John Booko, for inspiring me to learn the Aramaic and Eastern traditions.

Dr. Davis Bunn, for his strong vote of academic confidence.

Dr. Ergun Caner, for his dynamic editing and confidence.

John Claire, my father-in-law, who thought of the title, and who as a prolific reader has contributed much to my critical thinking over the past twenty-six years.

Dr. Eldon Clem, for his careful analysis of the Semitic words used in this book.

Doug Coe, for teaching about the *real* Jesus.

Drs. David Coffey and Ida Glaser, for their constructive critique and support.

Doug Fike for his faithfulness as a friend and the remarkable journey we are on together, as brothers, couples, and families.

My personal "core of companions," who pray and share joys and struggles together: Rev. Gary Bergel, Eric Fellman, Bud Harper, Rob Maffett, John Nakamura, Eric and Donna Sanson, and Dr. Dan Wolf.

Joseph Cumming, for his academic insights.

Dr. James DeFrancisco, for his insight into the Aramaic.

Harman Dudd (1912–2007), lifelong mentor and encourager of positive thinking.

Former Senator Ed Fredricks, who has been my associate and friend for over two decades, providing vast biblical insight.

Fr. Sidney Griffith, for his linguistic and moral contribution.

Dr. David Hungerford, for his unending editorial and financial support.

Dr. Pat Mercer Hutchens, for her scholarly advice on the Hebrew language.

George Kettle, for rallying behind me at critical times.

Terry Kingsly, for her constant urging to move forward in writing about these discoveries.

Samir Kreidie, for demonstrating what a "Muslim who follows Jesus" looks like.

Jim Lawler, for his lifelong friendship and for constantly pushing me forward.

John David Mann, for his brilliant editorial skills, dissecting countless hours of tapes, discussions, and pages of material, and translating them into cogent and compelling text.

Nassim Matar and his late wife, Maha, steadfast friends who patiently supported my work.

Margret McBride at the Margret McBride Literary Agency, and Michael Maudlin at HarperOne, for their tireless efforts to champion this project and help bring this story to light.

Dr. Ben and Katherine Meares, for their nonstop support.

Dr. Seyyed Hossein Nasr, for his detailed scholarly insight and attention to the manuscript.

Mark Powers, for his steadfast friendship and faithfulness over many years.

Joe Reeder, a prominent Washington attorney, for his friendship and personal help in editing the manuscript, and for securing edits from the eminent Islamic scholar Dr. Seyyed Nasr.

Dr. Hythem Shadid, who has supported the work for years.

Cal Thomas, for challenging me to persevere in seeking the truth.

Several sitting and former members of the U.S. Congress, for their encouragement over many years: Robert Aderholt, Tony Hall, Jim Inhofe, Joseph Pitts, Jim Slattery, Bob McEwen, Frank Wolf, and Zach Wamp.

Notes

CHAPTER 1: HOSTAGE
1. Soviet Jews who were refused emigration to Israel.
2. The U.S. hostages in Iran were formally released into U.S. custody on January 20, 1981, within twenty minutes after Reagan's inaugural address.
3. Short for "neoconservatives," a political movement that had emerged in the 1970s and established its first real political stronghold during the Reagan years.
4. Jerry Falwell, *60 Minutes*, October 6, 2002.
5. Benny Hinn, speaking at the American Airlines Center in Dallas, Texas, June 29, 2002.
6. Franklin Graham, *NBC Nightly News*, November 16, 2001.

CHAPTER 2: PARADIGM CRASH
1. *The Hollow Men* (1925).
2. Except where otherwise noted, all biblical passages in this book are taken from *Holy Bible from the Ancient Eastern Text, George Lamsa's Translation from the Aramaic of the Peshitta* (San Francisco: HarperSanFrancisco, 1985), for reasons explained in the next chapter.

CHAPTER 3: THE SECRET LANGUAGE OF THE BIBLE
1. Although I would not learn this until later, the Aramaic version of the New Testament also holds a unique importance for Muslims. Just as Muslims consider only the original Arabic-language version of the Qur'an the true, "Holy" Qur'an, because this was the language in which the text was first revealed to the prophet Muhammad, they likewise would consider

the text of the New Testament "Holy" only when written in the language of Jesus's original revelations—which would have been Aramaic.

2. Quoted here for purposes of comparison from the New King James version.

3. This is in fact exactly how the George Lamsa translation of the Aramaic New Testament, discussed later in this chapter, translates this passage: "It is easier for a rope to go through the eye of a needle, than for a rich man to enter into the kingdom of God."

4. Again, this is precisely how the George Lamsa translation of the Aramaic renders this passage: "He who comes to me and does not *put aside* his father . . ." However, in his *Language and Imagery of the Bible,* G. B. Caird maintains that "hate" is in fact the correct translation—but that this is a classic example of Aramaic hyperbole, whose literal meaning is something more like, "Unless he loves me more than his mother or father . . ." In other words, whether by dint of literal translation or cultural context, both scholars arrive at the same meaning through the Aramaic.

5. "Peshitta" is Aramaic for *straightforward,* perhaps suggesting that its creators felt it was more consistent with the original and not corrupted, as in the Western-language versions.

CHAPTER 4: THE OTHER HOLY BOOK

1. See Appendix 1, "Jesus in the Qur'an: A Complete List of Qur'anic References to Isa (Jesus)."

2. The Aramaic form, *qiriana,* reinforces the striking similarity of the languages.

3. Throughout our text, we use the names "Jesus" and "Isa" more or less interchangeably.

4. All passages from the Qur'an are taken from the English translation by Abdullah Yusuf Ali (Elmhurst, NY: Tahrike Tarsile Qur'an, 2005).

5. William M. Arkin, "The Pentagon Unleashes a Holy Warrior," *Los Angeles Times,* October 16, 2003. A Pentagon investigation concluded in 2004 that Gen. Boykin had violated regulations by failing to explain that he was not officially representing the government with these views, but no disciplinary action was taken.

6. From an address delivered to the Herzliya Conference, Lauder School of Government, Diplomacy and Strategy, December 17, 2003, as reported on Pat Robertson's official Web site: www.patrobertson.com/Speeches/IsraelLauder.asp.

7. In preparing this book for publication, I was no longer able to locate my source for this particular survey; however, I see similar national surveys, with similar results, cropping up at least several times a year.

CHAPTER 7: THE PATH OF ANANIAS
1. J. D. McAuliffe, *Encyclopedia of the Qur'an*, vol. 3 (Leiden, The Netherlands: Koninklijke Brill, 2005), 12.

CHAPTER 8: MY APOLOGY
1. When Qaddafi first seized power back in 1969, he accepted a ceremonial promotion from captain to colonel, and he has insistently remained at this rank ever since.
2. See their Web site at www.freedomhouse.org.
3. Remarks on Introduction of "The Apology for Slavery Resolution of 2000," by Rep. Tony Hall (D-Ohio), June 19, 2000.

CHAPTER 9: FULL CIRCLE
1. An imam is essentially the head of a mosque, just as a pastor is head of a church congregation.

CHAPTER 10: PILLARS AND BRIDGES
1. Genesis 15:6, quoted in Romans 4:3, Galatians 3:6, et al.
2. While an *imam* is essentially the Muslim equivalent of a pastor, a *sheikh* is more like a bishop, exercising a broader authority; the term can also refer to a tribal chief in the Arab world.

CHAPTER 12: JESUS, THE RUHALLAH
1. James Strong, *The New Strong's Exhaustive Concordance of the Bible* (Nashville, TN: Thomas Nelson Publishers, 1990), 49.
2. There is also an Arabic word, *eyal*, that corresponds to this idea.
3. Quoted here from the New King James version, because this entire verse is absent in the Lamsa edition. In fact, many scholars note that it appears only in fairly late manuscripts and believe it may have been a later addition to the original.
4. Muslim historian Jamal al-Din ibn Wasil, writing in 697.
5. The root word in Aramaic for "dead" is *m-t*. When Allah/God says on the day Adam ate the fruit he would surely die, the Aramaic (from the Targum) for the verb "die" is *tamoot*; elsewhere, "die" is *m-eet* and "death" is *motah* (e.g., in Deuteronomy 33:6). This appears to correspond to the Arabic word used in the Qur'an for Isa's state after his death: *motah*. The Coptic word for death is also very similar to the Arabic and other Semitic words: *Mooyt*.
6. Note that sura 19:15 uses the same wording to describe the death of John the Baptist. There has never been any doubt or controversy about this meaning "death" in this context, so why should there be any when the precise same terminology it applied to Isa?

7. *Tawaffa* occurs twenty-four times in the Qur'an to mean "death," and twice to mean "sleep."

CHAPTER 14: JIHAD

1. Avi Jorisch, in private conversation.
2. John L. Esposito, *Islam: The Straight Path* (New York: Oxford University Press, 1998), 59.
3. The words *rahman* and *rahim,* translated here as "benevolent" and "merciful," actually both derive from the same root, RHM (ر ح م), meaning "mercy," suggesting an even stronger emphasis on the idea of mercy as fundamental to the Qur'an's understanding of the nature of Allah.
4. Dr. Fr. Sidney Griffith, in private conversation.

CHAPTER 15: SCRUTINY

1. "Messianic Jew" is a term describing Jews who acknowledge Jesus as the Messiah foretold in Judaic tradition and at the same time continue to adhere to the practice of Judaism as their personal faith.
2. The resulting paper is scheduled to be published some time in 2008.
3. I had presented lectures to several hundred professors and students at the conservative Lancaster Bible College and Philadelphia Bible Seminary and had seen quite a few paradigms crash. But I had not presented my ideas to any major Evangelical Christian leaders.

CHAPTER 16: ON THE GREEN LINE AGAIN

1. Malcolm Gladwell, *The Tipping Point: How Little Things Can Make a Big Difference* (New York: Little, Brown, 2000).

CHAPTER 17: PATH OF PEACE IN A TIME OF WAR

1. Ori Brafman and Rod A. Beckstrom, *The Starfish and the Spider: The Unstoppable Power of Leaderless Organizations* (New York: Penguin, 2006).
2. Fareed Zakaria, "Mao & Stalin, Osama & Saddam," *Newsweek,* September 18, 2006.
3. "Koranic Duels Ease Terror," *Christian Science Monitor,* February 4, 2005.
4. Strictly speaking, the term "Messianic Muslim" is something of a tautology: because the Qur'an identifies Jesus clearly as "Messiah," mainstream Muslims, unlike mainstream Jews, already acknowledge Jesus as the Messiah who will return on Judgment Day. I use the term in a broader sense, to describe Muslims who have embraced a broader, more inclusive view.
5. Franklin Graham, *NBC Nightly News,* November 16, 2001.

APPENDIX 3: EXAMPLES OF ARAMAIC TERMS THAT
CLARIFY LONG-STANDING BIBLICAL MISINTERPRETATIONS

1. See Dr. George Lamsa's translation of the New Testament and his commentary, *Gospel Light: A Revised Annotated Edition* (Martinez, GA: Aramaic Bible Society, 2002), 82.

2. For a comprehensive discussion on the lineages of Matthew and Luke and the meaning of the Aramaic words translated as "husband" and "father," see Dr. Andrew Gabriel Roth, *Ruach Qadim: Aramaic Origins of the New Testament* (Malta: Tushiyah, 2005), 66–91.

Index

Index